curries
without
worries

an introduction
to indian cuisine

by sudha koul

"Remarkable little book"
CASHMIR INC.
Pennington

For Shyamji
"Something is better than nothing."

Koul, Sudha.
    Curries without Worries : an introduction to Indian cuisine /
by Sudha Koul. — Pennington, N.J. : Cashmir, c 1989.

    iv, 141 p. : ill. ; 20 cm.

1. Cookery, Indic.   I. Title
    TX724.5.I4K68 1989   641.5954—dc20   89-190022
                                                          AACR 2 MARC

Library of Congress

1991 Printing

Perfect Bind   ISBN 0-9624838-1-8
GBC Bind   ISBN 0-9624838-0-X

Address inquiries to:

CASHMIR
P.O. Box 111
Pennington
New Jersey 08534

Just a word . . .

I would never have written a cookbook if I had not come to live in the U.S., and had no choice but to do the cooking myself. If my friends had not shown so much interest in the Indian meals I prepared for them, if my husband had not looked after the children while I typed upstairs, if Vinnie Ogra had not let me borrow her typewriter, if Agha Shahid Ali had not played Professor Higgins, I would not have ventured on this project. I certainly would never have completed it were it not for Charles Burt, connoisseur of Indian food and onetime resident of India, who told me that I should write this book and found the time amidst his various, more important tasks to guide me. It was his wife, my friend Betty, who gave me the necessary courage from day-to-day by applauding whatever snatches I read to her. And last but not least, I would like to thank Donna Brugman for all the time and help she gave me during the final preparations of this book.

All these things have come to pass and the book has been written. I hope it makes some contribution towards satisfying the growing curiosity of American housewives about Indian cuisine. If it does, its purpose will have been served. The reader, particularly one with no prior experience in Indian cooking, will be well advised to go through the whole book before trying out the recipes. I hope that the informal, chatty style I have attempted will make the task relatively painless.

Sudha Koul

Pennington, 1983

This edition of "Curries without Worries" would not have been possible without a great deal of help from Beth Huskamp, Kamla Koul, and Jeannine von Ballmoos.

Sudha Koul

Pennington, 1989

CONTENTS

CURRIES WITHOUT WORRIES —
A SYNOPSIS

Introduction: In this chapter I describe what an Indian meal consists of and how it is to be served. My intention is to show the reader that preparing an Indian meal is quite simple. Some common misconceptions are dealt with and rectified. There is a discussion on spices, utensils, and other important requisites for Indian cuisine. I also explain why and for whom the book was written.

Basic Recipes: Recipes for GARAM MASALA, GHEE and Plain Yoghurt to start you off!!

Rice: I must confess that I was surprised to learn that most Americans consider preparing rice from scratch to be tricky. Keeping this in mind, I have given you detailed, easy-to follow recipes and tips that should make every reader eager to cook rice. The recipes range from plain to lavish . . . all simple, and simply delicious!

Breads: Indian breads are unforgettable for one reason: there is nothing else like them.

Usually made with wheat flour, they are utterly tasty. From amongst the staggering variety of Indian breads, I have chosen three of my favorite basic bread recipes.

Non-Vegetarian: Curries, roasts, KABABS—they are all here and simplified beyond belief! Cuts and sizes of meat are specified, leaving as little as possible for the cook to figure out.

Vegetarian: There is an infinite number of ways to prepare vegetarian food on the Indian subcontinent. Making a selection was difficult. I settled on the most popular recipes. Hopefully, this will be an incentive to vegetarians to add to their growing repertoire of recipes.

RAITA: A yoghurt-based vegetarian delight, RAITA is a natural food lover's dream-come-true. Always very popular with my friends here, it lends itself elegantly to innovation.

Salads, Chutneys, and a Pickle: For the adventurous, I have included simple recipes for Indian chutneys. Indian salads are quite unadventurous compared to their Western counterparts. They are meant to complement curries and to serve as a contrast to them. This they do superbly. My mother's Southern pickle recipe is thrown in as a bonus!

Desserts: Someone once described Indian sweets as confections "concocted from milk that has simmered and thickened for a couple of months at least." This is a slight exaggeration! Most Indian sweets are made from KHOYA, which is a milk solid formed from simmering and thickening milk for a few hours! I hasten to add that the recipes here are dependable shortcuts to a sweet finale, requiring neither months nor even hours to prepare.

Snacks: So good you may want to serve them as entrees! However, they are usually served at tea time.

Menus: A list of possible combinations for a complete Indian meal is given at the end of the book.

INTRODUCTION

Most Americans seem to know what a Chinese, or Mexican, or Middle Eastern meal looks like. However, when it comes to Indian food, most people have a vague impression of an entree called curry, which contains mysterious ingredients and is too hot. Fortunately, this impression is changing. The number of Indians living in this country has grown tremendously, and there has been a great surge of interest in all things Indian. In fact so many Americans have fallen in love with Indian cuisine that some of the ingredients used in Indian cooking have become quite commonplace. Indian restaurants have blossomed everywhere and are patronized by an increasing number of Americans who ooh and aah over the food, and not because it is too hot! Naturally, fascination with the cuisine has led to a desire to cook Indian food at home.

I still remember the day when some very dear friends of my husband invited us for dinner and served an Indian meal. They had, on occasion, enjoyed Indian meals cooked by my husband and wanted to give his still quite new bride a surprise. And they did! I had come to the U.S. for the first time and was intrigued by the prospect of eating an Indian meal cooked by Americans. To my surprise they served a delectable looking vegetable curry and hot, fluffy rice . . . a simple and authentic Indian meal. I eagerly took a mouthful and bit into something hard and pungent, almost bitter. The quintessential Indian spice turmeric . . . in its natural state! Swallowing it rapidly, I thought to myself that the recipe must not have explained that ground turmeric was required. I cannot think of any spice used in Western cooking that would even approximate such a culinary disaster had it been added whole instead of ground.

Even a cookbook must be inspired, and this episode sowed the seeds of a desire to introduce my new friends to Indian cooking. I hope my relating this episode at the very beginning of the book will not make an apprehensive reader even more apprehensive. I must add that, after removing the remaining pieces of turmeric, I enjoyed a hearty and delicious meal. The food was not rich, heavy, overly spicy or gourmet, rather, it consisted of wholesome, honest-to-goodness, everyday Indian preparations, thoroughly enjoyable and healthy, despite the aforementioned oversight. I was made to feel at home by the thoughtfulness that had gone into its preparation and by its superb quality.

A number of excellent books on gourmet Indian cooking are available in the U.S. However, I find that the appetite for Indian food has overstepped the confines of gourmet clubs; people want to prepare the Indian equivalent of steak and potatoes or spaghetti and meat-balls. Well, now you can do it, with this friendly little book for which you have been waiting!

I bought a Chinese wok a long time ago. With the wok came a little booklet containing a few recipes for Chinese preparations. This book has proven to be of greater use to me than some bulky Chinese cookbooks I own. Why? Because it is an uncomplicated introduction to Chinese cooking. It contains simple, but authentic and delicious, recipes which encourage you to try your hand at them. In my opinion, a lack of such an introduction to Indian cuisine is a justification for writing an Indian cookbook for beginners. The reader might still ask why one should bother with ordinary fare while preparing a meal intended to be exotic. The answer is that the flavors, appearance, indeed the whole experience, of an Indian meal—be it ever so simple—are in themselves exotic. Most people who try Indian food, even everyday fare, come back for more. Once you develop a taste for Indian food, you come to appreciate an entirely new culinary dimension. You cannot eat only gourmet dishes to fully appreciate the unique world of Indian cuisine.

It is not difficult...
the utensils are not elaborate...

At the risk of being barred from gourmet clubs, I must let you in on a secret. Most Indian dishes are simple and can be prepared in a short time. Cooking over open fires, as was the custom, hardly improves the flavor unless the recipe specifically calls for grilling. The pressure cooker is used often in Indian cooking now. I sense a disinclination to use the pressure cooker in this country. I shall consequently stick with pots and pans that pressurize neither the food nor the cook!

The best pots and pans for Indian cooking are heavy-bottomed, stainless steel saucepans or skillets. Non-stick pans are good for many things, but not for "browning" meats and vegetables, which is an integral aspect of Indian cooking. Stainless steel cooking spoons with long handles are best suited for Indian cooking.

For deep frying and for a host of other cooking procedures, Indians also use a type of wok called KADHAI. The KADHAI is heavier than most "oriental" woks and is superior for deep frying. This is because most Indian foods that are deep fried require the oil to be consistently very hot during the frying process, and hence, a heavy wok is preferable. However, if you do use the lighter wok, please regulate the heat.

Another Indian utensil indispensable for making breads is the TAWA or flat, heavy griddle. A cast-iron pancake griddle is an excellent substitute.

For making Indian breads, it is a good idea to buy a one-piece rolling pin of smaller diameter than the common pastry rolling pin. Rolling pins meant for pastry consist of two pieces. This is not efficient for Indian breads which are rolled out much thinner than pastry. The best utensil is an Indian rolling pin, called a BELAN, which is perfectly suited for rolling out Indian breads. (See Figure 1, page 46.) You can find the BELAN in an Indian store.

"Curry" defined...

What is a basic Indian meal? As I mentioned earlier, the Indian equivalent of an everyday American meal would be hot rice and/or bread with steaming curry. To avoid confusion between hot (as in steaming hot) and hot (as in spicy hot), I shall call the former hot and the latter spicy.

This is a good place to bring up an old worry that most people have about Indian food; i.e., that it is too spicy. This is a myth that needs to be exposed! For a country that takes five alarm chilli, jalapeno, hot chinese mustard, or Japanese radish sauce in its stride, Indian food is a bowl of cherries! The comforting fact about Indian food is that its ingredients can almost always be altered to suit the palate. It is not like a souffle that won't rise or a cake that won't bake. If you want to reduce the amount of spiciness in your cooking, you may do so. If, on the other hand, like a colleague of my husband, you don't feel you have had Indian food until you've used up all the tissue paper in the house, that is your privilege, and you may add pepper to your taste. NO recipe in this book is for a lethally spicy dish.

This brings us to THE QUESTION: what is a curry? I must mention here a discovery I made recently. There are some people who think that curry is a spice that grows on plants, like peppers or cardamons. Consequently, they say that they like to cook their food with curry. That is like saying you like to cook with souffles. A curry is a stew-like preparation of meats and/or vegetables, which is eaten with hot rice and/or bread. It is similar to meatballs in sauce on spaghetti. However, please note that if the curry is served with breads, it is not placed on top of the bread, rather, it is served on the side.

The curry may be very dry or may have a lot of gravy. Some people use the word "sauce," but I think gravy is a better word since it is formed from the juice of the meat or vegetable. A sauce is prepared separately, and lacks the essence of the meat or vegetable. A good rule of thumb is that curries eaten with breads have a thickish gravy and those eaten with rice have a gravy that is a bit thinner. Remember also that vegetables taste better with a thicker gravy, whereas meat and poultry make rich juices that permit thinner gravies.

Meats usually give out some moisture when they are cooked slowly. This results in the gravy being a bit thinner than I like it to be. To remedy this, I simmer the curry uncovered until I achieve the thickness I want. You can do the same.

The driest form of meat preparation is the TAN-DOORI, or roast, style. The meat is marinated in spices and yoghurt, but the marinade is almost completely absorbed during the cooking process. However, Indian curries must always be eaten with rice or bread. Even TAN-DOORI entrees are served with some form of bread, usually a yeast bread called NAN.

In some parts of India, breads called CHAPPATI or ROTI or PHULKI are more popular than rice. In fact, they form the staple. However, in most regions of the country, whether breads are served or not, rice is almost always served. Rice may be cooked plain or as a PULLAO (pilaf); i.e., with vegetables and/or meat. Similarly, breads may be simple or elaborate.

So far we have three items on our menu: curry, rice and bread. The fourth, and equally indispensable, item is DAL, or lentils. DAL is the major source of protein in India, particularly for vegetarians. A DAL does not look very different from lentil soup, although the cooking process is different. In any case, a well-cooked DAL is delicious enough to make you forget about animal protein! Supermarket lentils work well in most DAL recipes. However, if a recipe requires a specific DAL, you may have to buy it at an Indian grocery or a natural food store.

Accoutrements...

A must at an Indian meal is yoghurt. It is believed to have all kinds of medicinal and therapeutic properties. It cools in the summer, calms upset stomachs and, in general, contributes to longevity. Yoghurt is usually eaten plain, but sometimes broiled, boiled, chopped, or grated vegetables or fruit are added, and the concoction is called RAITA. I find that this is a particular favorite with my American friends. This is also a preparation with which an imaginative cook can innovate in infinite ways.

In Indian cooking yoghurt always means plain yoghurt. Even a yoghurt mildly flavored with vanilla is "out."

Invariably, an Indian meal includes a salad of some kind. Those who cannot afford a fancy salad have a chopped onion and/or a hot green pepper along with their meal. In middleclass homes, a salad (pronounced SALAAD) usually consists of very finely chopped or sliced vegetables tossed together and sprinkled with salt, pepper, and fresh lime juice or vinegar. Only a few vegetables are used for salads, and the attitude toward experimentation is rather conservative.

Finally, we come to the condiments, or little palate teasers, which for some people, are an indispensable part of an Indian meal. These are PAPADS or PAPPADOMS, chutneys, and pickles.

PAPADS are a lentil-based, tortilla-like cracker which can be crumbled into rice and curry, or nibbled before dinner as an appetizer. The preparation of PAPADS is better left to the commercial manufacturers and certainly does not need to be included in a beginner's cookbook. Any Indian store stocks a good variety of PAPADS.

Chutneys have been immortalised in the Western world, particularly in the U.K., by Major Grey, and quite a good selection is available here. However, what often passes for chutney belongs more to the realm of preserves. Fresh chutneys, more common in India, are

12

quite different from preserves in texture and taste. Preserves are usually sweet and, more often than not, made with lime or mangoes. However, fresh chutneys may be made of mouth-watering combinations of mint, coriander, dates, tomatoes, peppers, walnuts, coconut or sour cherries. Chutneys are incredibly easy to prepare, and I have included a few recipes.

Indian pickles, called ACHAR, are usually based in mustard oil and are very spicy, very tangy. They may take some getting used to! Every region has its folklore about which area makes the deadliest pickles. Some pickles are allegedly so spicy and peppery that one spoonful burns right through the rice to the plate. One hesitates to think of what it might do to one's alimentary canal. Food for thought?

The fact remains that making Indian pickles at home is a bit complicated. Fortunately, pickles lend themselves very nicely to bottling and Indian stores stock excellent pickles of the highest quality. I have given you a simple recipe for one of my favorite pickles. This pickle is not available in stores.

Sweetmeats, called MITHAI in India, are often served at high tea or at festive occasions. However, at an Indian meal, you may or may not be served dessert. It depends upon where you are in India. When dessert IS served, it is traditionally an Indian equivalent of a rice pudding, called KHIR or PAYASAM or FIRUINE. Since most Americans find a meal without a dessert to be incomplete, I have included a few choice recipes for MITHAI.

Curry explained...

So there you have it, the mystery of what makes up a typical Indian meal is unravelled! A few further explanations are in order. The fare served to the Moghul emperors of India was, no doubt, far more intricately designed and served than are the meals at my mother's house in India. However, rich food, even if it is MOGHLAI, is not something you can have every day without considerable damage to your well-being. "MOGHLAI" cuisine is now the speciality of restaurants and is far richer than everyday Indian cooking, although the latter is influenced by the former. Besides, as I have mentioned earlier, quite a few excellent books have been written on gourmet Indian cuisine. It is the wonderful range of delicious and light everyday Indian cookery that has been neglected. This book seeks to fill that void.

I often recall the story my American sister-in-law told me about the first time she had an Indian meal. At the time, she had no idea that she would one day marry an Indian. She had gone to Toronto with friends who loved Indian food. They could not persuade her to try it. Finally, they decided that she should wait for them to eat, and she would eat later at another restaurant. While waiting for them to finish their meal, she nibbled at a piece of TANDOORI chicken, and the rest, so to speak, is history. I will not let Indian cookery take the credit for her later decisions in life, but I will certainly say it was a case of coming to scoff and remaining to pray. They left the restaurant much later than planned. This kind of conversion is more the rule than the exception, and it is for friends like her that I am writing this book.

Curry Universal...

One more diversion before we get on with the recipes. There is no national Indian cuisine. Just as Chinese cuisine varies from province to province, so does Indian cooking. Since I am from the north of India, my recipes are a bit biased in that direction. However, most of the recipes in this book are those that have gained popularity all over India. These are also the dishes most familiar to Americans who frequent Indian restaurants.

I have stayed away from dishes that require the technical expertise of those who can whirl pizza dough into the sky and successfully retrieve it. In short, I have introduced you to the kind of fare you would have at my mother's house and at the houses of my friends all over India. This book contains tested and tried recipes from relatives and friends, and their names go with the recipes. I have made some modifications in order to further simplify procedures.

The ingredients...
readily available

The other day in a book store, I overheard a lady talking to the sales clerk. She had just bought a gigantic book on Asian cookery and was complaining that the bigger task was yet at hand; i.e., procuring spices and utensils. Indeed, when you look at an Indian cookbook for the first time, it may look as though every recipe is complicated, because it calls for so many ingredients. The fact is, that once you have a "starter kit" of spices, you

15

will use the same ingredients again and again in different combinations. I remember that when I came to the U.S., I had to go out and stock up on oregano, parmesan, rosemary, thyme, parsley, tarragon, black pepper, white pepper, Worcestershire sauce, basil, sage, chives, spaghetti, tartar sauce, baking soda, baking powder . . . I could go on and on. Indian cooking IS a different cuisine, but once you have obtained the basic spices and utensils I have described, you are set to explore a wonderful new subcontinent of food! It may come as a surprise to you that the crucial spices for most Indian dishes can all be found in the average supermarket, sometimes in the gourmet section.

There are a few spices used in Indian cooking which are not yet readily available in American supermarkets, such as asafoetida (called HING in India). Even minute quantities of this resin-like substance produce an unique aroma. However, when I moved to our new house in New Jersey, I was miles away from an Indian grocery, and I did very well without HING. In fact, no one noticed its absence. I can see a lot of fanatical eyebrows go up at that sentence! If you insist, you can buy it at the local Indian store. I assure you that HING is not to Indian food, what dough is to pizza.

Tamarind, another important ingredient, particularly for South Indian cooking, is readily available only in the Indian groceries. It is the sour pulp of the fruit of the tamarind tree and when added to a preparation it imparts to it a tart flavor, brownish coloring, and something appetizingly undefinable.

Now we come to the question that you have so patiently waited to ask. What about curry powder? This is one thing almost everybody knows about. When curry powder is added to fricasseed chicken, for example, the chicken is, by common consent, converted to curry. By inference, anything with a dash of curry powder qualifies as a curry. Not so! Indians do not use curry powder as it is known in the West. Using a single combination of MASALAS (spices) for all curries is unheard of. It is as unthinkable as using the same herbs for all Western dishes. Most Indian homes use a blend of spices, called GARAM MASALA, for a final garnish. I have given you a recipe for GARAM MASALA, which is also excellent for TANDOORI meats. Of late pre-mixed spices for different dishes have become available even in India (a boon for working women!) Convenience is probably one explanation for the origin of curry powder. Some packaged varieties of premixed spices are available in the Indian grocery stores or gourmet sections of some supermarkets here.

Seasonings I use fresh are:

Coriander
Curry leaf (similar to bay leaf, just adding curry leaf
    does not make a curry)
Garlic
Fresh ginger
Hot green peppers or "chillies"
Mint
Onions
Scallions

In orthodox Indian households dry MASALAS are

ground freshly every day. However, in the homes of those of us who have no desire to spend most of our lives in the kitchen or to hire someone just to pulverize spices, dry spices, whole and ground, can be bottled and stored in separate jars.

The dry seasonings on my shelves are:

Asafoetida (HING) ... powdered or in small lumps
Black pepper .... whole and ground
Black cardamon .... whole, crushed
    (BADI ILLACHI)   or ground
Black cumin seeds .... whole
Bay leaves .... whole
Cardamon .... pods or seeds; whole, crushed
                                or ground
Cayenne pepper .... ground
Cinnamon .... whole, crushed or ground
Cloves .... whole or ground
Coriander seeds .... crushed or ground
Curry leaves .... whole
Cumin seeds .... whole or ground
Fennel seeds .... whole or ground
Fenugreek seeds .... whole or ground
Ginger .... ground to a powder
Dry hot red peppers .... crushed or whole
Mustard seeds .... whole, sometimes ground
Nutmeg .... grated or ground
Onion Seeds .... whole
Turmeric .... ground

18

NOTE: Turmeric is beneficial to your system, but its stains are difficult to remove. So, be careful while using it.

I hesitate to include saffron in either herbs or spices, since it is quite delicate, extraordinary and in a class by itself. Perhaps, being a native of Kashmir, which has the most spectacular saffron fields in the world, I have a special feeling for saffron.

I also have a great partiality for fresh coriander, called DHANIA in India. It looks like parsley, but the similarity ends there. It adds a fantastic dimension of flavor and fragrance, to Indian food. It is also used in Italian, Armenian, Mexican and Chinese cooking. In the last couple of years I have been able to find it quite easily in the supermarkets here. It is wonderful to see these changes. I grow mine in the summer, by soaking a handful of coriander seeds in a cup of water overnight and sowing them the next day. It takes about a couple of months to become identifiable as coriander, but it is worth the wait to me!

So, this is the assortment I have on my kitchen shelves, and it comes, almost entirely, from supermarkets. I will not dispute the fact that this is not a complete list of Indian spices and herbs, but it will suffice for most people who cook Indian food. At any rate, I have managed fairly well with this list and have found my way to my husband's heart and to the hearts of some friends. They have never questioned the authenticity of my preparations!

You can be assured that all the recipes in this book are truly Indian. The only exception, I must confess, is the Mango Souffle which I have included because it is simple, unusual and delicious.

This book is an attempt at helping West meet East. The meeting place is not in the recipe, which is purely Indian, but in the enjoyment of the cuisine.

The cooking medium ...

In India, mustard seed oil, coconut oil, sesame seed oil, peanut oil, etc. are used in different regions. I find corn oil a perfect (also healthy) substitute for all of these, since it does not have an intrusive flavor.

Clarified, strained butter, or GHEE, is also used in India. Regular butter works just as well, but if you do use butter instead of GHEE, melt it first on low heat, before you heat it up for the recipe. Otherwise it might burn. If you want to use GHEE, which has a richer flavor than butter, you can make it at home. The method is simple and is given in the basic recipe section. For the sake of convenience, I shall use the word GHEE in the recipes, unless butter is specifically called for.

A final word on ingredients ...

Be sure to have a supply of dry nuts such as almonds, walnuts, pistachios and cashews, as these are used in many special dishes.

Curry served ...

How is an Indian meal to be served? The traditional

method is to serve food on a THALI, or large metal plate of either silver, brass or stainless steel. The rice is placed in a little heap at the center, and the dishes are served in very small bowls (or KATORIS) set around the rice. Very rarely is a meal served course by course. In modern households, THALIS and KATORIS have been replaced with smaller china or stainless steel plates. The serving dishes are placed at the center of the table, as they are here, and passed around for people to help themselves.

I can anticipate the next questions. How do you help yourself? What comes first? The usual procedure is to take a small helping of rice or bread in the center of your plate and then to place the various entrees and accompaniments around it. If you prefer, you may take a small serving of rice with one entree, then a second serving of rice with another entree, and so on. Or, you may eat rice or bread with all the entrees. There are no hard and fast rules. Small bowls for DALS or curries with a lot of gravy are very good substitutes for the KATORIS used in India. Your guests can place their bowls on the sides of their plates, and help themselves with a teaspoon.

Vegetarians should be particularly delighted to see how balanced, nutritious, and delicious an Indian vegetarian meal is. The variety of vegetarian dishes from India is practically infinite. I should point out that if vegetables done Indian-style appear overcooked, it is because Indians are wary of undercooking their vegetables. You can always improvise and cook vegetables to the degree of tenderness you prefer.

Another thing to keep in mind is that "vegetarian" in India means the total absence of meat, fish, chicken, egg, or the stock or flavoring thereof. This is due to

personal or religious reasons. Our family is non-vegetarian, and sometimes I add stock or bouillon to vegetarian recipes instead of water. Of course this is only
when I am not entertaining vegetarian friends. It seems
to add a little something to the flavor, but that may just
be the prejudiced view of an avid non-vegetarian!

I have given you a list of possible menus for Indian
meals at the end of the book. There are no stringent rules
for determining combinations, only those dictated by
taste.

When shopping . . .

Always buy fresh lamb. If your local supermarkets
do not have a good selection of fresh lamb, try a farmer's
market. When you buy lamb and have it ground, it is a
good idea to ask the butcher to trim all the fat before
grinding it. Ground turkey is readily available now, and
it is being touted as the healthiest form of ground meat.
I use it almost all the time and find it a lean and healthy
substitute for ground lamb without any of the flavor one
normally associates with turkey. In fact, it is so lean that
I sometimes add a spoonful of corn oil to it. In any event,
unless I inform my guests, they always assume they are
eating either ground beef or lamb. It's quite amazing.

Indians do not, by and large, eat beef. However most
Americans prefer beef to lamb, and you may substitute
beef for the lamb recipes. Quite a few Indians here do
that, and they tell me that if the cut of beef is lean and
tender, there is hardly any noticeable difference in taste.

When shopping for chicken, try to buy the smallest
variety; i.e., fryers or Cornish game hens. The smaller the

chicken, the better suited it is to Indian cooking. This could be due to the fact that large birds cannot absorb the spices as well as the smaller birds can.

A great variety of fish is available in India; brook trout in the north in Kashmir, river and lake fish in the mainland, and a plentitude of seafood in the vast coastal areas to the south.

For the recipes I have given you, a mild, white fleshed fish such as flounder, catfish, halibut, orange roughy, cod, or sole is the best choice.

Although frozen peas are indispensable, in general, the results are much better when you use fresh vegetables.

IMPORTANT: HAVE ALL YOUR INGREDIENTS READY BEFORE YOU COOK. IF YOU HAVE OIL HEATING ON THE BURNER, THERE MAY NOT BE ENOUGH TIME TO GO LOOKING FOR CUMIN SEEDS, OR TO START CHOPPING ONIONS!

Let's try some recipes now!

BASIC RECIPES

GARAM MASALA

1 large cinnamon stick, or 2 medium sticks, coarsely crushed
1 tablespoon whole cumin seeds
1 tablespoon coriander seeds
1 tablespoon peppercorns
1 tablespoon cardamon seeds
1 tablespoon cloves
1 tablespoon fennel seeds
1/2 teaspoon grated nutmeg

Preheat the oven to 350 degrees for 10 minutes. Spread out all the spices, from cinnamon to nutmeg, in a single layer on a cookie sheet. Place the cookie sheet in the oven for 20 minutes until the aroma of toasted spices begins to emanate. Remove from oven, and cool completely at room temperature. Then, grind spices together in a blender until all the spices are reduced to a powder. The cinnamon may be a little coarse, but you can sift the spices and grind the coarse pieces again. This yields about 1/2 cup. You can store the MASALA in a tightly capped bottle for future use. It should keep for several months. This book has many recipes that require this MASALA. If you plan to make these recipes often, it is a good idea to double or triple the amount of MASALA you make and store it.

GHEE

Melt and simmer a pound of unsalted butter in a very heavy saucepan at the lowest possible heat until a clear, yellowish liquid forms on top and almost all the sediment from the butter has settled at the bottom. This should take about 15 minutes. Cool to room temperature. Strain, and pour into a jar that can be covered tightly. Any foam still floating at the top can be removed by straining. The main point is that when a clear, yellowish liquid has formed from the butter, and some sediment has settled at the bottom, the GHEE is ready. Any further simmering may cause the GHEE to burn and turn into a brown liquid, which is not what you want. The GHEE should keep for many months.

Plain Yoghurt

    1 quart whole milk
    2 tablespoons plain yoghurt

Bring the milk to a boil in a 6-quart saucepan. Stir to prevent overflow when the milk starts to boil. When milk starts to boil, lower heat to lowest point possible, and simmer for 10 minutes.

Allow milk to cool for about half an hour. It should be very warm when you put your finger in to test it, but not so hot that you cannot put your finger into it comfortably.

Next, mix the yoghurt with 2 tablespoons of the milk and mix well into the rest of the milk.

Cover with a lid and wrap in a very thick towel or cloth. Keep undisturbed in a draft free place overnight.

Remember:

1. Once you place the yoghurt to set, do not disturb!

2. If the yoghurt turns out watery or sour it means the milk was too hot when you mixed in the culture.

3. If the yoghurt does not form, the milk was not warm enough or the culture was too mild.

4. Yoghurt takes less time to form in warm weather.

The way to check whether it has formed is to lift the lid and blow on it. If it has not set, cover and keep for a few more hours undisturbed.

RICE

There are two basic ways to cook rice.

1. Plain, i.e., boiled with water

2. Cooked with other ingredients

   When other ingredients are added to rice, it may be cooked as a BIRYANI, PULLAO or KHICHDI. I have given you basic recipes for these variations. These dishes are quite rich and can be eaten with only a RAITA or a salad as an accompaniment. However, other entrees can be included for grander feasts.

Keep in mind:

1) Regular long grained rice takes a little longer to cook than BASMATI rice.

2) Stir the rice only before the grains have become tender, or else the grains will break and the rice will become lumpy.

Plain Boiled Rice

Serves 2

6 cups water
1 cup long grained rice

Bring water to a boil on high heat in a 4-quart saucepan. Add the rice, stirring constantly. Lower the heat to medium and cook for 15 minutes, stirring once or twice to prevent the rice from sticking to the bottom of the pan. When the rice starts puffing up, drain off the water in a soup strainer. Transfer the rice back to the saucepan, lower the heat to the lowest point and cover the saucepan. Cook for 5 minutes. Serve hot. It is safer to cook rice with less water. If you use too much to start with, there is no way out. However, if after following the instructions above, the rice is not tender enough, add 3 tablespoons of water, cover and continue to cook on the lowest possible heat for another 5 minutes. Add the water by pouring it over the rice, as you pour syrup over pancakes. Do not stir.

Leftover rice is best re-heated by steaming.

If you prefer to cook the rice without draining off the water, this is the method:

1 cup rice
2 cups water

Bring the rice and water to a boil on high heat and continue to boil for 2 minutes, stirring off and on to prevent the rice from sticking to the bottom of the pan. Reduce heat to the lowest point, cover, and cook for about 15 minutes, until the rice is puffy and tender. If the rice appears a little hard after following the above procedure, pour 3 tablespoons of water over it, cover and cook on the lowest heat for another 5 minutes.

Serve hot.

Vegetable PULLAO

Serves 4

4 tablespoons GHEE
1 medium sized onion, chopped
1 teaspoon very finely chopped fresh ginger
1/2 teaspoon ground turmeric
3 cloves
2 small sticks cinnamon
2 bay leaves
2 cardamon pods, coarsely crushed
1/2 teaspoon whole cumin seeds
1/2 cup frozen peas
1-1/2 cups cubed or chopped vegetables, i.e. potatoes, cauliflower florets (fresh or frozen). You may use other vegetables of your choice, provided they are cut into small pieces and are of the crunchy variety. Squash, pumpkins, or leafy vegetables should not be used in a PULLAO.
1 cup long grained rice, preferably BASMATI
2-1/2 cups water. If this is not a vegetarian vegetable

PULLAO, you could substitute stock or bouillon for the water. This is to be added in place of the water, not in addition to it.

salt to taste

a pinch of saffron, soaked in 5 tablespoons of water

Heat the GHEE in a 4-quart saucepan on high heat for 1 minute. Add the onion, ginger and turmeric, and fry for 1 minute. Add the cloves, cinnamon, bay leaves, cardamon pods and cumin seeds. Stir well to prevent burning and sticking to the pan. Fry for a few seconds. Add the vegetables, and stir fry for 2 minutes. Add the rice, and stir briskly for a few seconds. Add the water (or stock) and salt, stirring constantly. When the entire contents of the saucepan begin to boil, reduce heat to the lowest possible point, add saffron with the water, stir, and cover. Cook for 15 minutes.

The vegetables may rise to the top, but do not stir after the rice has started boiling, as this will cause the rice to break and become lumpy.

Serve hot.

Nana's Lamb BIRYANI

Lamb, rice, tomatoes and saffron in a rich BIRYANI

Serves 6

8 tablespoons GHEE

3 large onions, chopped

2 tablespoons chopped fresh ginger
2 cloves garlic, minced
2 lbs. lean fresh leg of lamb, cut into 2" x 2" x 1" pieces
1 teaspoon ground cayenne pepper
1/2 cup yoghurt
2 medium tomatoes, finely chopped
4 cardamon pods, crushed
2 cinnamon sticks
8 cloves
3 bay leaves
salt to taste
8 cups water
2 cups long grained rice, preferably BASMATI
peels from 2 quartered oranges
12 bay leaves
1/2 cup blanched peeled raw almonds
a good pinch saffron, soaked for an hour in 1/2 cup water
2 tablespoons butter, cut into small cubes

Heat the GHEE in a 6-quart saucepan on high heat. Add the onions, ginger and garlic, and stir fry until reddish. Add the lamb, and stir fry till it turns a golden brown. Take care that the lamb does not stick to the pan and burn. Stir occasionally to prevent this. However, stirring too often prevents the lamb from browning. This part requires the utmost attention of the cook.

When the lamb is nicely browned, reduce the heat to medium high.

Add the cayenne pepper, yoghurt, tomatoes, cardamon, cinnamon and cloves; fry for a couple of minutes. Add the bay leaves and salt; bring to a boil. Cover; reduce heat to low; and cook for half an hour. Set aside.

In a separate saucepan, bring 8 cups of water to a boil. Add the rice; stir; and continue to boil on medium high heat for 5 minutes. Drain off all the water in a soup strainer. Set rice aside.

Line the bottom of a 4-quart saucepan with the orange peels (inside up) and the bay leaves. Spoon a layer of rice on the peels and bay leaves, enough to cover them. Next, add a layer of the cooked meat without the gravy, using a slotted spoon. Now, spoon another layer of rice on the meat, and repeat until you have layered all the rice and meat. The top layer should be rice. Spoon the gravy (from the meat) in a circle on the edge of the rice. Scatter the almonds on top, in the center. Pour the saffron with the water inside the ring of gravy. Now, if the BIRYANI is seen from the top, it should have almonds in the middle, a ring of saffron around the almonds, and a ring of gravy around the saffron. Dot the top with the butter cubes. Cover the saucepan, and cook the BIRYANI on the stove top on the lowest heat for about half an hour.

Serve hot.

When you serve the BIRYANI, remove the orange peels and bay leaves.

Mom's Popular Lamb PULLAO from Kashmir

Serves 4

2 lbs. lean sliced shoulder of lamb, each slice divided into
    two pieces
3 cups water
1 teaspoon ground turmeric
1/2 teaspoon ginger powder
1 teaspoon ground fennel seeds
5 cloves
salt to taste
6 tablespoons GHEE
6 bay leaves
1 cup long grained rice
a good pinch of saffron
3 tablespoons yoghurt
3 cardamon pods, crushed
1/2 teaspoon ground cumin seeds
1 stick cinnamon
1 cup sliced onions
3 tablespoons oil
3/4 cup raw almonds and/or cashews
3 hard boiled eggs, sliced

Place the meat in a 6-quart saucepan. Add the water,
turmeric, ginger, fennel, cloves and salt. Bring to a boil;
reduce heat to low, cover, and cook for half an hour. With
a slotted spoon, remove the meat from the gravy, and
set aside. Measure and set aside the gravy.

Heat the GHEE on high heat in a 6-quart saucepan. Add
the meat and bay leaves, and fry until the meat is crisp

35

and golden brown. Reduce heat to medium.

Add the rice to the meat. Stir fry briskly, until the rice is well fried. This should take a few seconds.

You will need about 2-1/2 cups of liquid for the rice to cook. If the gravy from the meat is 2-1/2 cups, add it to the rice. If it is less, add water to make 2-1/2 cups. In either case, use only 2-1/2 cups.

Stir. Add the saffron, yoghurt, cardamon, cumin, and cinnamon; stir well. Bring to a boil. Cover, reduce heat to the lowest point, and cook until the rice is tender and puffy. This should take 15-20 minutes.

Fry the onions in oil on medium high heat until reddish and crisp. Remove with slotted spoon. Set aside.

Fry the nuts until golden. Remove with slotted spoon. Set aside.

When ready to serve, spoon PULLAO onto an oval platter. Scatter the onions on top, and edge the platter with the fried nuts and sliced eggs.

Serve hot.

KHICHDI with Moong and Meat, or, Real Kedgeree

Americans are familiar with moong beans, the source of bean sprouts. Whole or split, moong beans are a perennial favorite in India and are used in innumerable dishes. Here moong is cooked with rice and meat to form a nutritious and delicious meal-in-one!

Serves 6

1 cup moong beans soaked for 6 hours in 4 cups of water
6 tablespoons GHEE
1 teaspoon whole cumin seeds
5 cloves
2 lbs. very lean lamb, cut into 2 inch cubes
1 teaspoon ground turmeric
salt to taste
4 cardamon pods, lightly crushed
2 cinnamon sticks
3 bay leaves
1/2 teaspoon ginger powder
2 teaspoons ground fennel seeds
3 more cups water
2 cups long grained rice

Drain and reserve the water from the moong beans. Set the moong aside.

Heat the GHEE on medium high heat in a 6-quart saucepan. Add the cumin seeds, and stir until they sizzle. Add the cloves and meat.

Brown meat well.

Add the turmeric, salt, cardamon, cinnamon, bay leaves, ginger powder and fennel. Stir briskly to fry all the spices and meat together for a few seconds.

Add 3 cups of water and the water from the beans to the meat. Stir, and bring to a boil. Reduce the heat to low, cover and cook for 20 minutes.

Remove from heat.

Drain and measure the gravy from the meat, and set it aside.

Return meat to stove top.

Add the rice and the moong to the meat. Stir fry on high heat for a few seconds. Next, add 4 cups of the gravy. (If there is not enough gravy, add water to it to make 4 cups of liquid.)

Stir; bring to a boil; cover; lower heat to lowest point; and cook this way for about 15 minutes or until the rice is done.

Serve hot.

BREADS

CHAPPATI: An everyday bread, also called ROTI or PHULKI, a CHAPPATI is rolled out round and flat, like a tortilla. Traditionally, it is toasted on a griddle and inflated on an open fire. The method given here is a simplified one, although the results are equally good.

PURI: Made with whole wheat flour and a little oil, a PURI is rolled out flat and round and then deep-fried. It should ideally puff up into a translucent, round shape when fried.

PARATHA: A layered bread, PARATHA is folded and rolled out flat into round, square, or triangular shapes. Made with whole wheat flour and either butter, or GHEE, or shortening, PARATHAS can be cooked like CHAPPATIS or fried like pancakes. And this is not all! One can make them plain or stuff them with vegetables or meat.

The CHAPPATI is the thinnest bread. The PURI is thicker, and the PARATHA is the thickest, particularly the stuffed type.

These are all non-yeast, everyday breads. It is, frank-ly, difficult to make very fine CHAPPATIS with the whole wheat flour that is available in most supermarkets. I feel that mixing whole wheat flour with all purpose flour, in half and half proportions, makes a very nice dough for all these recipes. If you are a devotee of whole wheat and will not brook any mixture, that is fine too. The breads are going to be a bit coarse, but will still be delicious. If you are a devotee of the authentic, then your local Indian grocery (and sometimes the Chinese) is a good source for "CHAPPATI" flour made from whole wheat. However, for the sake of convenience I shall refer to the flour used as whole wheat flour, and leave the choice of what you use to you. All purpose white flour is not recommended.

All Indian breads are eaten hot off the griddle. You can make them ahead of time and keep them warm or re-heat them in the oven. This is a good place to make the point that kept coming to mind while I was trying and testing the recipes for this book. It is AMAZING how heat levels differ in both cooking ranges and griddles. The main thing to remember while making the breads is that the griddle should not be so hot that the bread gives off a burning smell the second you start to cook it. It is far better for the heat to be a little low than too high. This is because the breads cook in a matter of seconds, or a couple of minutes, at the most. The other thing to keep in mind is that sometimes even the most seasoned (and regular) cook of Indian food has to sacrifice the first CHAPPATI or PURI or PARATHA to test the waters. You have to get an idea of how hot the griddle or the cooking range is, and one CHAPPATI or PURI or PARATHA is a small price to pay.

CHAPPATIS, as taught by Pichi

Makes ten CHAPPATIS, each about 4-1/2 inches in diameter

1/2 cup cold water
> (You may need a teaspoon or two more, or less, than 1/2 of a cup of water. This is because, like cooking ranges, cup sizes differ, and in small amounts that little difference can make a big difference!)

1 cup whole wheat flour

a small bowl of extra flour for patting down and rolling out the CHAPPATIS

Add the water to the flour, a little at a time, and mix well. Knead well until a soft, but not sticky or wet, dough is made. This should take a few minutes. (If you are using a food processor, follow the instructions to make dough.) The dough should tear easily when you pull a piece off. Cover with a damp cloth, and let it rest for an hour prior to cooking. This improves the consistency of the dough. When you are ready to make the CHAPPATIS, roll the dough into a "log", approximately the shape of commercially prepared frozen cookie dough. Cut into 10 portions as you would for cookies (Figure 2, page 46). Roll each portion into a ball, using the palms of your hands and moving them in a circular motion as you would if you were applying lotion to your palms.

Place the ball in the extra flour; press it down in the center with three fingers, first on one side, then on the other. Now it will look like a patty.

Next, on a flat surface, roll out a CHAPPATI to about the same thickness as a tortilla and about 4-1/2 inches in diameter. If you roll it out much more than that, it may not inflate well.

The art of rolling out a CHAPPATI is to be mastered. If your first CHAPPATI bears a striking resemblance to the map of the United States, do not be disheartened. You may be surprised to see how near perfect your next CHAPPATI will be.

One way of rolling out the CHAPPATI is to first roll out a slightly elongated piece, then turn it around, so that the narrow side is rolled out, making it round. You can repeat this process until the CHAPPATI is roundish and has a diameter of about 4-1/2 inches. The CHAPPATI has to be rolled out a little at a time. If you roll out one side too long, you may tear the CHAPPATI and will then have to roll it into a ball and start all over again.

You may add a little flour to facilitate the rolling. I find that, compared to other flours, all purpose flour makes rolling out very easy. (You should dust off the extra flour by blowing on the CHAPPATI before you place it on the griddle.) Acquiring an Indian rolling pin, as stated earlier, will make the task of rolling out CHAPPATIS much easier. Applying a gentle pressure, roll out the CHAPPATI in a backwards and forwards motion, till you have a nice round shape. If I could learn to do it, you certainly can!!

Roll out all the CHAPPATIS at the same time so that you can cook them one after the other, instead of having to stop and roll them out one at a time.

Cover the rolled out CHAPPATIS with a damp, muslin type of cloth to prevent them from drying out before cooking. The important thing is that you spread them out on a counter or tray: DO NOT PLACE THEM ON TOP OF EACH OTHER. Otherwise, you might find that they have turned into a solid mass. I had this nightmarish experience once, and never fail to pass this tip on to my friends.

If, on the other hand, you plan to roll out the CHAPPATIS one at a time, cover the dough with a light, damp cloth while you do the toasting.

When you are all set to cook the CHAPPATIS, heat a pancake griddle, or TAWA, on medium heat for at least 10 minutes. Reduce the heat to low. It was difficult to agree upon exact times and temperatures for breads that are cooked in a jiffy, but I have tried to be as exact as I possibly could. The important thing to remember is that it is better to have the heat low than high. A little experience is the best guide in this matter.

When you think the griddle is right to toast the CHAPPATI gently, place the CHAPPATI in the center of the griddle.

After half a minute, when the CHAPPATI changes color all over, lift with a spatula and turn over. Toast the bread on the other side for half a minute. Turn over. With a small hand towel (folded twice), gently press the edges of the CHAPPATI down. It will start inflating. Then very gently, press the center down so that the CHAPPATI inflates into a roundish, puffed bread. This should take about a minute. Now the CHAPPATI is ready to be served.

Some people like to brush their CHAPPATIS with a little butter or GHEE at this stage. Do not be disheartened if the CHAPPATI does not inflate as promised. Continue to follow the procedure, and it will cook properly. Taste the first CHAPPATI to see where you stand.

With a little experience, you will improve by leaps and bounds. Wipe the griddle between CHAPPATIS (to remove leftover dry flour) with a damp cloth. A delicious aroma will fill your kitchen as the aroma of freshly baked bread will do. The CHAPPATI is not a yeast bread, so this aroma is different, but just as appetizing.

Serve hot.

PARATHA

Ideal for Improvisation! You can make it plain, or stuff it with vegetables. Even if you make it plain, you may add a pinch each of all, or any, of the following to the flour prior to making the dough: salt, anise seeds (whole or ground), whole fennel seeds.

Plain

Makes 5 Plain PARATHAS

1 cup whole wheat flour
about 1/2 cup water (as with CHAPPATIS, see page 42)
About 5 teaspoons GHEE, melted
a small bowl of extra flour for rolling out PARATHAS
about 3 teaspoons extra GHEE for crispy style PARATHAS

BELAN
Figure 1

"COOKIE" ROLL
Figure 2

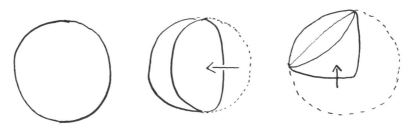

TRIANGULAR PARATHA
Figure 3

(NOTE: A word about the GHEE. There is no exact amount essential to the formation of a PARATHA. I have indicated approximate amounts. You may like more or less. Or you may not want GHEE at all. In that case, butter-flavored vegetable shortening is a good substitute. Oil is not a good medium for PARATHAS. Shortening, butter, or GHEE are the best.)

When preparing the dough, follow the same procedure as you would for CHAPPATIS, up to the point at which you cut the pieces for the balls. Since PARATHAS are thicker than CHAPPATIS, you must cut 5 pieces instead of 10. When rolling out the PARATHAS keep the same instructions in mind for the dough that you do when rolling out the CHAPPATI . . . spread them out, cover them, etc.

PARATHAS can be made in the following shapes:

Triangular (Figure 3, page 46): Make a ball of the dough as you would for the CHAPPATIS and flatten it with three fingers. Pat both sides down in the extra flour. Then, on a flat surface, roll out the flattened dough ball into a round shape about 4 inches in diameter. Place 1/4 teaspoon GHEE in the center and spread it gently with your finger tips, well within the outer edges of the rolled out dough. Pick up one edge of the round and bring it over the other side, so that you have folded it in half, with the GHEE side inside. Now you have a half moon shape in front of you. Then fold the half moon in two, making it into a triangular

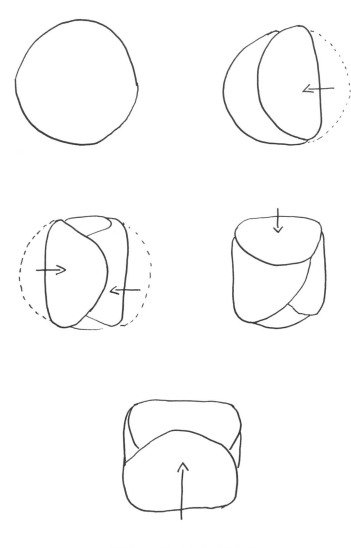

SQUARE PARATHA
Figure 4

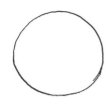

Rolled out dough   Side view   With stuffing

Gather edges
above stuffing

Fold & press
together

Press down

STUFFED PARATHA
Figure 5

**PANCAKE GRIDDLE
WITH
DOMED SAUCEPAN LID**
Figure 6

shape. With the help of a little flour, roll out a triangular PARATHA with all sides the same length, about 5-1/2 inches. Use the principle of rolling out a little at a time so that all sides are rolled out evenly, using a backwards and forwards movement.

Square (Figure 4, page 48): Follow the procedure for triangular PARATHAS up to the stage at which you have spread the GHEE in the center. Then, take one edge and bring it down over the GHEE, a little inside the edge (as shown in the picture). Press down gently. Repeat with the opposite side and press down this edge over the previously folded edge. Repeat with the top and bottom, so that you have folded it like a square envelope, although the folds will overlap a great deal more than do the folds of an envelope. All these folds make the PARATHA layered, quite light and delicious. With the help of a little flour, roll out one side at a time, until each side is about 5-1/2 inches and you have a square-shaped PARATHA.

Round (Figure 5, page 49. Instead of stuffing you will place GHEE inside.) Follow the same procedure as for triangular PARATHAS up to the point at which you have spread the GHEE in the center. Then, lift all the edges, and press together over the GHEE portion, pressing hard with your fingers to make them stick together, forming a pouch with the GHEE inside. Press the pouch down and with the help of a little flour roll out into a round PARATHA about 5-1/2 inches in diameter.

So much for the shape. Now for the taste. Depending

on your preference, you can make PARATHAS soft or crisp.

SOFT STYLE: Heat a pancake griddle on medium heat for 10 minutes. Reduce heat to low. Place the PARATHA on the griddle. After a minute, flip it over. Take care to regulate the heat so that the PARATHA cooks well and does not burn outside or remain undercooked inside.

Cook for another minute and flip it over again.

Cover the PARATHA with a domed lid from a saucepan (Figure 6, page 49). The dome need not be higher than an inch. This way you form a mini oven in which the PARATHA is well cooked inside and out. A friend of mine taught me how to make grilled cheese sandwiches like this. Cook this way for half a minute on either side.

You have first toasted the PARATHA and then baked it. Remove from griddle and set aside after brushing half a teaspoon GHEE on top. When you make the next PARA-THA, place it on top of the first PARATHA, on the side on which you had brushed the GHEE. Then brush the GHEE on top of the second PARATHA. Repeat this procedure till all the PARATHAS are made. Indians do not mind having their PARATHAS "buttered" on both sides!

CRISP STYLE: Follow the above procedure up to the point where you are to cover the PARATHA with a lid. Instead of covering the PARATHA with a lid, pour 1/2 teaspoon of GHEE around the PARATHA, just as you would with pancakes. Lift the PARATHA for a second with a spatula, so that the GHEE spreads evenly on the underside. After half a minute, flip the PARATHA over and repeat the procedure with the GHEE.

You have first toasted the PARATHA and then fried it on both sides.

It is a good idea to check the first PARATHA to be sure of the time required to cook it. If you feel the dough inside is undercooked, prolong the toasting stage by half a minute on both sides.

You must taste the first PARATHA to get a good idea of the heat and time required for cooking. All this sounds quite complicated. However, once you have done it, it is as simple as frying an egg. If you were to learn about frying eggs from a cookbook without ever having seen them being cooked, the instructions would be as detailed! When you fry PARATHAS, there may be some spattering and smoking from the GHEE. Remember always to wipe the griddle with a damp cloth after making each PARATHA to remove any flour that may remain on it.

Serve hot!

Stuffed PARATHA a la New Delhi

These are PARATHAS stuffed with grated fresh cauliflower and spices. You may substitute finely minced onions or boiled, drained, coarsely mashed potatoes, and add the seasonings indicated for the caulifower. The essential thing to remember is that the stuffing should be absolutely dry, without liquid or gravy, or else the PARATHA will not seal properly when you make a pouch of it. A stuffed PARATHA is usually crisp outside and soft inside. I know of few things that make a winter's day come alive so well as a well-made stuffed PARATHA and pickles.

To make 4 stuffed PARATHAS

Stuffing

1 cup grated cauliflower
1 tablespoon grated fresh ginger
half a cup chopped fresh coriander
1 finely chopped medium sized onion
1/4 teaspoon ground cumin seeds
1/4 teaspoon ground coriander seeds
salt to taste

To make dough

1 cup whole wheat flour
about 1/2 cup water (as with CHAPPATIS, see page 42)
1/8 teaspoon ground anise seeds
a small bowl of extra flour for rolling out breads
8-10 teaspoons GHEE

Mix all the ingredients for the stuffing well and set aside for an hour at room temperature. Make the dough for the PARATHAS with the flour, water and anise. The method is the same as that for CHAPPATIS. Set aside for an hour at room temperature before preparing the PARA-THAS.

When ready to make the PARATHAS, squeeze the water from the stuffing and drain. The stuffing should be as dry as possible.

Next, follow the procedure for making CHAPPATIS up to the point at which you have to cut the dough roll. Since stuffed PARATHAS are thicker than plain PARATHAS, cut the roll into 4 pieces.

Then, make 4 balls of the pieces of dough, as you would for CHAPPATIS. Flatten each ball with three fingers, and pat down both sides on the extra flour. Then, on a flat surface, roll out the flattened dough ball into a round shape, about 4 inches in diameter. Place 1/4 teaspoon GHEE in the center and spread it gently with your finger tips, well within the outer edges of the rolled out dough.

Next, take one fourth of a cup (or enough to close the pouch comfortably) of the stuffing and place it in the center of the circle, taking care to see that the edges are free of GHEE and stuffing. Fold by picking up all the edges of the circle and pressing them together above the veg-etables, making a pouch as you would for the circular PARATHA (Figure 5, page 49). You may have to pull up the edges a bit. Press the edges together hard to make them inseparable. Gently flatten the pouch with the tips of your fingers, and sprinkle a little flour on top of it. Turn over and sprinkle some flour on the other side, too. Turn it over again so that the "pressed-together" side will be up. Gently applying the least possible pressure, roll out the PARATHA to about 5-1/2 inches in diameter. Sprinkle a little more flour on the PARATHA, if necessary, to prevent tearing. The stuffed PARATHA is about twice as thick as the plain PARATHA, but it is the same diameter.

If you plan to make the PARATHAS all at the same time,

spread them out on a tray to prevent them from becoming one solid mass.

When ready to cook the PARATHAS, heat a pancake griddle on medium heat for about 10 minutes. Reduce the heat to low and place the PARATHA on it.

After one minute, turn over and cook on the other side for one minute. Turn over and cover with a lid, and cook this way for a minute on both sides.

For soft PARATHAS, proceed as you would for soft plain PARATHAS. For crisp PARATHAS, fry as you would for crisp plain PARATHAS.

Serve hot!

Saryu's Alltime PURIS

Puffed, deep fried breads

Makes 12

    1 cup whole wheat flour
    1/2 cup water, approximately, as with CHAPPATIS (page 42)
    a pinch of salt
    2 cups oil for deep frying the PURIS
    a few teaspoons of extra oil for rolling out the PURIS

Mix all the ingredients, EXCEPT the last two, well. Knead until the dough becomes stiff. This should take a few minutes, less in a food processor. The dough should not be elastic; rather, it should tear when you pull a piece off.

Set aside for a couple of hours at room temperature.

When ready to fry, make a roll and cut it into 12 pieces. (See CHAPPATIS.)

Make balls of the 12 pieces as you would for CHAPPATIS. Spread a few drops of oil on the counter and then roll out the PURIS. With the help of the oil, roll out the PURIS into flat round shapes about 3-1/2 inches in diameter. Follow the same method for rolling out the PURIS as you would for CHAPPATIS, with the difference that you will use oil instead of flour.

Prepare all the PURIS beforehand, since it takes only a jiffy to fry them once the oil is ready. Remember to spread them out on a tray and cover them as you would the CHAPPATIS, as you will fry the PURIS one at a time.

Heat 2 cups oil in a wok on high heat.

It is crucial that the oil for deep frying the PURIS be at the right temperature, i.e., very hot, otherwise they will not inflate. A well fried PURI is almost round like a ball. A little experience in this, as in all else, is the best guide. Whatever you do, please use common sense in regulating the heat. The oil should be hot, but not dangerously so!! One method of checking whether the oil is hot enough, is to put a pinch of dough into the wok. If it rises to the top, sizzling, the oil is ready.

When you think the oil is ready, slide one PURI into it, without splashing the oil!

Pour oil continuously onto the PURI from the sides so that it is being fried from above and below. The PURI should fry briskly. If the oil just simmers without any change in the appearance of the PURI, the oil is not hot enough.

Fry the PURI for about 15 seconds on one side. Turn over carefully with a slotted spoon and fry for about 5 seconds. Lift with the spoon and hold it above the oil for a couple of seconds to drain off excess oil. Transfer to a large bowl or tray lined with paper towels. The towels will soak up the excess oil from the PURI.

The first PURI should give you a good idea of the time required to fry the PURIS. It should be a light, or golden, brown. Fry all the PURIS the same way, and transfer them to a paper lined dish.

PURIS can be eaten with vegetables and DALS and go particularly well with potato curries.

Serve hot or cold.

NON-VEGETARIAN

Chicken Curry a la Mussoorie

This creamy chicken should melt in the mouth

Serves 6

2 medium onions, coarsely chopped

4 cloves garlic

1 tablespoon chopped fresh ginger

2 tablespoons water

3/4 cup GHEE

1 teaspoon whole cumin seed

2 small frying chickens, cut up
(The elimination of pieces with bone reduces the flavor
of a curry considerably. You could substitute thighs and
drumsticks if you like, but avoid using boned breast of
chicken. Remove skin, and clean chicken with dry paper
towels before cooking.)

1 teaspoon ground turmeric

1/4 teaspoon ground cayenne pepper

1/2 teaspoon ground cumin seeds

1 teaspoon ground coriander seeds

6 crushed cardamons

1 cinnamon stick, medium size, crushed

2 bay leaves

salt to taste

a pinch of nutmeg

1 pint sour cream

2 tablespoons blanched slivered almonds

1 cup chopped fresh coriander

Puree the onions, garlic, ginger and 2 tablespoons of
water, in a blender.

In an 8-quart saucepan, heat the GHEE on medium high heat. When the GHEE is hot, add the whole cumin, stirring briskly until the seeds sizzle. Add the puree and continue to stir. Regulate the heat to prevent the puree from sticking to the bottom of the pan, which it has a tendency to do. Continue stirring till the puree is golden, has been fried well, and most of the moisture in the puree has evaporated. This will take about 10 minutes on medium high heat.

Add the chicken. Stir fry on high heat till the chicken starts turning golden brown. This should take about 5 minutes. Stir fry briskly to prevent burning the chicken. Add the turmeric, cayenne pepper, cumin, coriander, cardamons, cinnamon, bay leaves, salt and nutmeg, stirring well until they give off a fragrance; i.e., for a minute or so. Add the sour cream, stirring constantly. Bring to a boil, reduce the heat to lowest point possible, cover tightly, and cook for 30 minutes or until the chicken is absolutely tender.

Just before serving, sprinkle almonds, and then fresh coriander, on the curry.

Serve hot.

TANDOORI Chicken

This is a spectacular way to serve chicken. For those who like it spicy, it can be spiced up by doubling, or tripling, the amount of red cayenne pepper.

Serves 6

2 whole, small frying chickens
1 medium sized onion, coarsely chopped
1 tablespoon finely chopped fresh ginger
4 cloves garlic
1/2 cup very thick yoghurt
1 teaspoon ground cayenne pepper
salt to taste
1/4 cup lemon juice
3 tablespoons GARAM MASALA
4 tablespoons GHEE

Remove the skin from the chickens. With a sharp knife, make 3 parallel slits on the fleshy parts. The slits should be bone deep and about 3 inches long. Do not worry if the chicken looks torn up. This way it absorbs the marinade better.

Puree the onion, ginger, garlic, yoghurt, cayenne pepper, salt, lemon juice and 2 tablespoons of the GARAM MASALA together in a blender. This is the marinade.

Rub the marinade into the chickens, well into the slits and the rib cage from inside, so that the chickens are completely marinated. Keep in the refrigerator overnight for the best flavor. If you are in a hurry, marinate for at least 10 hours!! In any case, you must turn the chickens a couple of times while marinating, so that they are well marinated inside and out, top and bottom.

Preheat the oven to 500 degrees for 15 minutes.

Place the chickens in a roasting pan or dish. Sprinkle the remaining GARAM MASALA on the birds, and place in the oven. After 10 minutes, lower the heat to 400 degrees, put 2 tablespoons of GHEE on each chicken; and cook for 50 minutes until done. Do not pour the leftover marinade on the chicken or even baste the chicken with the marinade, since that will make it soft. TANDOORI chicken has to be crisp. That is why the oven has to be really hot to singe and seal the chicken and to prevent the juices from flowing out. Traditionally, TANDOORI chicken is made with a whole chicken, but if you prefer, you can use thighs and drumsticks. Naturally these take less time to cook than a whole chicken, but the temperatures required for cooking are the same.

Serve at once!!

PIAZ Chicken

Chicken in onion gravy

Serves 6

5 tablespoons oil
4 cups chopped onions

6 small chicken legs and thighs (12 pieces, if cut at the joint)
8 cardamons, crushed well
2 medium cinnamon sticks
salt to taste
1/3 cup water

Heat oil in a 4-quart saucepan on high heat. Add the onions, and fry until golden. Add the chicken. Fry until the chicken begins to brown a little. Add the cardamon and cinnamon, salt and water. Stir well, lower heat to medium, cover, and cook for about 20 minutes. Then remove the cover, turn up the heat to high, and stir and cook until the liquid is reduced to a thickish gravy. This should take a few minutes.

Serve hot.

Whispering Windows Butter Chicken

Chicken cooked with a buttery gravy ... a very popular restaurant item

Serves 6

12 chicken thighs
1 cup yoghurt
salt to taste
1/4 lb. butter
1 big onion, finely minced
1-1/2 teaspoons ground cumin seeds
1-1/2 teaspoons ground coriander seeds
1-1/2 teaspoons ground cayenne pepper

1 cup strained tomatoes
1/2 cup heavy cream
1/2 cup cashew nuts, ground
1 teaspoon cardamon seeds, crushed well

Remove skin from chicken. Make 2 parallel slits in each piece. Marinate overnight in yoghurt and salt.

When ready to cook, heat the butter in a 6-quart saucepan on medium high heat.

Add the onion and stir fry till golden, but not brown. Add the cumin, coriander, cayenne pepper, tomatoes; stir well. Add the marinated chicken, with the marinade. Reduce heat to medium. Stir. Cook covered for 15 minutes.

Add the cream, cashews and cardamon; stir well. Cover and cook for 45 minutes, stirring occasionally.

Serve hot.

White Rondo a la Turk SHAMI

Rounds of ground turkey (or lamb), cooked in a delicately seasoned yoghurt gravy

Serves 6

2 lbs. finely ground turkey or lamb
1 teaspoon cardamon seeds
salt to taste
1 tablespoon ground fennel seeds
2 teaspoons ground cumin seeds

1-1/2 teaspoons ground coriander seeds
2 tablespoons oil
2 teaspoons ginger powder
6 cloves
1-1/4 cup of water
4 tablespoons oil
1 cup chopped onion
1 tablespoon finely chopped fresh ginger
1-1/2 cups yoghurt
a pinch of saffron, soaked in a tablespoon of water
1/4 teaspoon cardamon seeds, powdered

Mix the following well: Ground turkey or lamb, cardamon seeds, salt, fennel, cumin, coriander, 2 tablespoons oil and ginger powder. Knead well for a minute or so. Divide into three equal portions. Make each portion into a roll about 6 inches long and about 2 inches in diameter, patting the rolls to help shape them. Place the meat "logs" or rolls in a heavy 6-quart saucepan. Add the cloves and water and bring to a boil over high heat. Cover, lower heat to medium, and continue to cook until the rolls are cooked and firm. This should take about half an hour. Remove from heat and allow to cool before placing in the refrigerator for a couple of hours.

When chilled, remove from the refrigerator. Remove the rolls from the saucepan. Reserve the liquid in the saucepan. Slice the rolls into half inch thick slices. Set liquid and rolls aside.

Heat the oil in a small frying pan, or saucepan, on high heat. Add the onion and fresh ginger, and fry until reddish. Add to the liquid in the saucepan.

Bring the contents of the saucepan to a boil.

Add the yoghurt, stir briskly. Add the slices of ground meat roll. Add the saffron.

Bring to a boil again. Add the powdered cardamon. Lower to medium, cover, and cook for 10 minutes.

Serve hot.

KOFTE/MACHH/Meatballs

Red hot meatball curry!

About 20 meatballs

2 lbs. lean ground meat
2 teaspoons ground cayenne pepper
5 tablespoons oil
1 teaspoon sugar
1 teaspoon ginger powder
2 teaspoons ground fennel seeds
1 tablespoon whole fennel seeds
1 teaspoon whole cumin seeds
1 tablespoon cardamon seeds
salt to taste
1 medium onion, chopped
4 cloves
1/2 cup yoghurt
1-1/2 cups water
1/4 teaspoon each: ground cinnamon, ground cardamon
    seeds, ground cumin seeds

Spread the ground meat on a large plate. Sprinkle 1

teaspoon of the cayenne pepper on the meat.

Heat 2 tablespoons of the oil in a small, heavy saucepan until it starts to smoke a little. Pour over the meat. Add the sugar, 1/2 teaspoon of the ginger powder, 1 teaspoon of the ground fennel, whole fennel, whole cumin seeds, cardamon seeds, and salt.

Knead together for a couple of minutes until all the ingredients are well mixed.

Now shape the meat balls. Traditionally, in Kashmir, these are made slightly elongated, like link sausages of a medium size. However, you could, if you prefer, make them round. Set meatballs aside.

Heat the remaining oil in a heavy 6-quart saucepan on medium high heat. Add the chopped onion and immediately thereafter the cloves; and fry till golden brown.

In the meanwhile, mix the remaining cayenne pepper well with the yoghurt. When the onions are a golden brown, add the cayenne pepper-yoghurt mixture. Stir fry briskly for a couple of seconds. Some rather pungent aromas emanate at this stage. People have been known to yearn for these aromas!!

Add the water, remaining ground fennel and ginger; stir briskly until the mixture boils.

Add the meatballs, one at a time. Reduce heat to low, cover, and cook for about half an hour or until the meat balls become firm and are well cooked and the oil has risen to the top of the liquid in the saucepan.

Once you have placed the meatballs in the saucepan, do not stir until they have become firm. You could lift the saucepan and gently turn it about so that the gravy spreads well around the meatballs, but this need not be done more than once, if at all.

Once the meatballs are cooked and are firm, stir gently. Sprinkle the ground cardamon, cumin and cinnamon on the meatballs; stir a little to mix well with the gravy; cover; and cook on low heat for another 5 minutes.

Serve hot.

Reheat on low heat till it starts simmering. It reheats deliciously.

KHULLA KEEMA

Ground meat cooked with eggs, peas and spices

Serves 6

1 medium onion, chopped coarsely
2 teaspoons chopped fresh ginger
4 cloves garlic
2 tablespoons water to blend onion, ginger and garlic
3/4 cup oil
1/2 teaspoon whole cumin seeds
2 lbs. ground meat (lamb, beef or turkey)
1 tablespoon ground cumin seeds
1 teaspoon ground cayenne pepper
2 tablespoons ground coriander seeds
1/2 tablespoon ground turmeric
20-oz packet of frozen peas
salt to taste

3 hard boiled eggs, halved
4 tablespoons heavy cream
1 teaspoons cardamon seeds, crushed
2 medium sticks cinnamon, crushed
1/2 cup water
1/2 cup chopped fresh coriander

Puree the onion, ginger and garlic and 2 tablespoons of water in a blender.

Heat the oil on high heat in a 4-quart saucepan. Add the whole cumin seeds, and stir fry for a couple of seconds. Add the puree, and stir fry till the puree acquires a golden color. Stir to prevent burning.

Add the ground meat and stir fry well, breaking up lumps, for about 5 minutes. Reduce heat to medium. Add the ground cumin, cayenne pepper, ground coriander, ground turmeric, peas, and salt. Stir fry for 2-3 minutes. Add the eggs, cream, cardamon, cinnamon and water. Stir well, cover, and cook on medium heat for about 20 minutes. Sprinkle fresh coriander on top and serve.

TIKKA KABABS

These are similar to shish kababs, so popular in the U.S., but the marinade is spicier.

Serves 6

2 tablespoons GARAM MASALA
2 tablespoons lemon juice

1 small onion
1 tablespoon chopped fresh ginger
5 cloves of garlic
1 teaspoon ground cayenne pepper, or more, to taste
salt to taste
4 tablespoons sour cream
2 lbs. boneless lamb, (preferably from butterflied leg of
    lamb), cut in 2 inch cubes

Puree all the ingredients, EXCEPT the lamb, together in a blender.

Pierce the cubes of lamb with a thick skewer or sharp knife, so that a visible hole is made in the meat. The idea is to allow the meat to marinate properly, which is the entire secret of this recipe. Marinate overnight in the refrigerator.

When you are ready to cook, place the KABABS in a broiler pan to drain off excess juices.

Heat the oven to a full broil for 15 minutes.

Place the KABABS in the oven. Broil for 15 minutes. Remove from the oven; turn pieces over. Broil for another 15 minutes.

Serve at once.

Sliced onions (marinated for a couple of hours in vinegar, a dash of cayenne pepper, and salt) are a good accompaniment. You may also serve a quartered lemon on the side of the KABABS, if you wish.

TANDOORI chicken and TIKKA KABABS can also be cooked

on an outdoor grill. However, outdoor grills being different, you will have to use a little independent judgement about time and temperature. I find that TIKKA KABABS taste more authentic when cooked on the grill.

My Mother-in-Law's YAKHNI for all Seasons

A mild, aromatic lamb curry

Serves 4

2 lbs. fresh lean lamb shoulder, sliced
2 cups water
6 cloves
1 teaspoon ground cumin seeds
1 teaspoon ginger powder
2 teaspoons ground fennel seeds
3 bay leaves
1 cup thick whole milk yoghurt
2 tablespoons sour cream
4 cardamon pods, coarsely crushed
salt to taste
1 tablespoon GHEE
1 medium onion, minced
1 tablespoon finely chopped fresh ginger
a pinch of saffron

In a 4-qt. saucepan, bring the lamb, water, cloves, cumin, ginger powder, fennel and bay leaves to a boil on high heat. Reduce the heat to medium; cover; and cook the lamb until it is tender. This should take about 35 minutes.

There should be about half a cup of water left when the lamb is finished cooking. A little more won't hurt, but if the water dries up while the lamb is cooking, add half a cup of water to it. Stir once or twice to ensure that the lamb does not stick to the pan and burn. Mix the yoghurt and sour cream. Add to the lamb; stir well, and raise heat to medium high. Bring to a boil. Add cardamon and salt. Remove from heat and set aside.

In a separate pan, heat the GHEE on high heat.

Add the onion and ginger, and stir fry until golden brown. Add to the lamb. Next, add saffron to the lamb; stir; cover; and cook lamb on low heat for about 10 minutes.

Remove the saucepan from the heat and let it rest for 5 minutes before serving.

YAKHNI improves in flavor if kept overnight! Re-heat on low heat till it starts simmering.

Serve hot.

Anu's Melt-in-the Mouth BHUNA Lamb

Lamb cubes cooked in a rich, aromatic marinade

Serves 6

2 cups yoghurt
8 cloves garlic
1 tablespoon chopped fresh ginger
1 teaspoon ground red pepper

1 teaspoon GARAM MASALA
1 teaspoon ground coriander seeds
1 teaspoon ground cumin seeds
2 teaspoons lemon juice
salt to taste
2-1/2 lbs. boneless lamb shoulder cut into 1-1/2" cubes
1 tablespoon oil

Puree all the ingredients, EXCEPT the lamb and oil.

Marinate the lamb in the puree for 4-5 hours in the refrigerator.

Place the meat, with the marinade, in a heavy 6-quart saucepan. Bring to a boil on medium high heat. Lower heat to medium, cover, and simmer for half an hour, until the lamb is tender.

Continue to cook uncovered until most of the moisture has evaporated and the lamb is thickly coated with the gravy. Add 1 tablespoon oil, and stir fry for 2 minutes.

Serve at once.

SAG GOSHTH

Meat Curry in a rich, melt in the mouth, creamy spinach puree

Serves 6

One 10-oz packet of fresh spinach
6 cups of water

1 large onion, coarsely chopped
4 cloves garlic
1 tablespoon chopped fresh ginger
2 tablespoons water
1/2 cup oil
8 cloves
2 lbs. lean lamb, such as lean sliced shoulder of lamb, cut
     into approximately 2" x 3" x 2" pieces
2 medium tomatoes, coarsely chopped
1 teaspoon ground cayenne pepper
1/2 teaspoon ground turmeric
1/2 teaspoon ground cumin seeds
1 cinnamon stick, coarsely crushed
1/2 cup sour cream
1/2 teaspoon cardamon seeds, crushed
salt to taste

Wash and drain spinach. Place spinach in a 6-quart saucepan. Add 6 cups of water. Boil for three minutes. Remove from heat. Cool.

Reserve the spinach and one cup of the liquid. Discard the rest of the liquid. Puree the spinach and the cup of liquid in a blender. Set aside.

Puree the onion, garlic and ginger with two tablespoons of water.

In a 4-quart saucepan, heat the oil on high heat. Add the cloves and the onion puree. Stir fry briskly for 2 minutes, until the puree starts turning brown. Add the meat, and continue to fry briskly for 2 minutes. Lower heat to medium high, and continue frying until the meat starts browning. This should take a couple of minutes.

Add the tomatoes, cayenne pepper, turmeric, cumin, cinnamon, sour cream, cardamon and salt. Stir fry well for a few seconds, and bring to a boil.

Add the spinach puree, stir. Reduce heat to the lowest point. Cover. Cook this way until the meat is tender. This should take about 45 minutes.

Serve hot.

KALIYA

Lamb pieces cooked with yoghurt and turmeric

Serves 4

2 lbs. lamb shoulder, sliced 2 inches thick
2 cups water
6 cloves
2 teaspoons ground turmeric
1 tablespoon ground fennel seeds
1/2 teaspoon ginger powder
1/2 cup yoghurt
salt to taste
3 tablespoons butter
1/4 teaspoon ground cinnamon
1/2 teaspoon ground cumin seeds
6 cardamons, crushed thoroughly

Divide each lamb slice into two pieces.

Bring the lamb, water, cloves and turmeric to a boil on high heat. Mix the fennel and ginger in the yoghurt. Add to the lamb. Bring to a boil again.

Add salt. Reduce heat to low; cover and cook for about 40 minutes. Set aside.

Heat the butter on high heat. Add the cinnamon, cumin, and cardamon. Stir. Add to the lamb mixture.

Cook lamb for another 10 minutes on low heat.

Serve hot.

ROGHANJOSH

The ultimate Kashmiri lamb dish, ROGHANJOSH is cooked in an aromatic red gravy made with ground red peppers and yoghurt.

Serves 4-6

1/2 cup oil
8 cloves
1 medium onion, chopped
3 lbs. leg of lamb, or shoulder, cut into chop-size pieces
1/2 cup yoghurt
1 teaspoon chopped fresh ginger
2 tablespoons ground cayenne pepper
3 cups water
1 tablespoon ground fennel seeds
1 teaspoon ginger powder
salt to taste
1/4 teaspoon ground cinnamon

1/2 teaspoon ground cumin seeds
8 cardamons, crushed well

Heat the oil in a heavy 6-quart saucepan on high heat for 3 minutes. Add the cloves and onion. Fry until the onion turns reddish. Add the meat. Fry until it starts to brown a bit. Add the yoghurt and ginger. Stir and fry, until the liquid from the yoghurt evaporates.

Remove from heat and quickly add the cayenne pepper; stir until the meat acquires a red color; add the water; and return saucepan to heat. Add the ground fennel, ginger and salt. Bring to a boil. Reduce the heat to low. Cover and cook until the lamb is tender. This should take about 45 minutes. If, after 45 minutes, the lamb is still not tender and the water has evaporated, add another cup of water and cook for another 15 minutes or until done.

When the lamb is tender, add the cinnamon, cumin and cardamon. Stir, cover, and cook for one minute.

Serve.

Shahi Mia's recipe for SHAHI KORMA

Spiced lamb legacy from the Moghuls

Serves 8

1/2 cup oil
2 big onions, sliced
2 tablespoons grated fresh ginger

5 cloves garlic, minced
3 bay leaves
4 lbs. lamb or beef cubes
2 teaspoons ground coriander seeds
1 teaspoon ground cayenne pepper
1/2 teaspoon cardamon seeds, powdered
1 teaspoon GARAM MASALA
salt to taste
1 cup well stirred yoghurt
1/2 cup blanched slivered almonds
1/4 cup heavy cream
a pinch of saffron soaked in 2 teaspoons water

Heat the oil in a 6-quart saucepan on high heat for 2 minutes.

Add and fry the onions, ginger, garlic and bay leaves until the onions are brownish.

Add the meat and fry till it starts to brown. Next, add the coriander, red pepper, cardamon, GARAM MASALA, and salt.

Stir fry well for a couple of minutes.

Add the yoghurt, stir, reduce the heat to low, cover, and cook until the meat is tender. This should take about half an hour.

Add the almonds, cream and saffron with the water; stir, cover and cook for another 5 minutes.

Serve.

AWADHI PIAZA

A courtly concoction of onions, meat, and spices

Serves 8

1/2 cup oil
2 lbs. sliced, not chopped, onions
8 cloves garlic minced
1-1/2" x 1" slice fresh ginger, chopped
1 medium tomato, chopped
20 peppercorns
10 cardamons, lightly crushed
2 large cinnamon sticks
10 whole dry red peppers
1 teaspoon cumin seeds, lightly crushed
10 cloves
salt to taste
3 lbs. lamb cubes, about 1-1/2" x 1" x 1" pieces
1/2 cup beaten yoghurt

Heat the oil in an 8-quart saucepan on high heat for a couple of minutes. Add the onions, garlic, and ginger; stir fry until nicely browned. Then add the tomato, and stirring all the time, cook for about 2 minutes.

Add all the other ingredients EXCEPT the lamb and yoghurt, and stir fry for another minute or so.

Add the meat, and stir fry for 5 minutes.

Add the yoghurt, stir, cover, reduce heat to medium, and cook until the meat is tender. This should take half an hour.

Serve.

An Everyday VINDALOO

A rich, peppery curry based in vinegar and freshly blended spices, Vindaloo is addictive! It is traditionally made with pork, but lamb and beef work just as well.

Serves 4-6

2-1/2 lbs. boneless pork, beef or lamb cut into 2" x 2" x
    1" pieces
6 tablespoons vinegar
2 large onions, sliced
2 tablespoons chopped fresh ginger
6 chopped garlic cloves
1 cup chopped fresh coriander
4 dry hot peppers
1 tablespoon whole cumin seeds
2 inch cinnamon stick, coarsely crushed
6 tablespoons oil
1 tablespoon ground turmeric
1 teaspoon ground black pepper
3 hot green peppers
salt to taste
1 teaspoon sugar
1/2 teaspoon ground cloves
2 cups water

Marinate the meat in 2 tablespoons of vinegar for 4 hours in the refrigerator.

Blend the onions, ginger, garlic, coriander, hot dry peppers, cumin and cinnamon with the remaining vinegar to make a paste. You may have to add a tablespoon or two of water to facilitate blending.

When ready to cook, heat the oil in a 6-quart saucepan on high heat. Add the puree, and reduce heat to medium high. Fry briskly for a couple of minutes.

Add the turmeric, ground black pepper, meat, and the marinade. Fry well for 10 minutes, taking care not to burn the meat. Stir briskly, constantly.

Add the green peppers, salt, sugar, cloves and 2 cups of water. Stir, cover, reduce heat to medium, and cook for about 45 minutes, until the gravy thickens and the meat is completely tender.

Serve hot.

Jigri and Buttons' Unforgettable Tandoori Fish

Serves 6

    1/3 cup vinegar
    1 tablespoon chopped fresh ginger
    4 cloves garlic
    salt to taste
    1 tablespoon ground coriander seeds
    1 tablespoon ground cumin seeds
    1 tablespoon ground cayenne pepper
    1/2 cup oil
    2 lbs. of any mild white fish fillets, cut into 2" x 3" pieces
        (I found that orange roughy and catfish work
        particularly well for this recipe.)

Make a paste of the vinegar, ginger, garlic, salt, coriander, cumin, cayenne pepper and oil in the blender.

Marinate the fish pieces in the paste for 4 hours in the refrigerator.

Turn the oven on to broil at the highest point. Place the fish pieces on a baking tray. Broil for about 10 minutes. Turn over on the other side, and baste with the liquid in the baking tray. Broil for about 7 minutes again.

Broiling time may differ, depending on the thickness of the fillets. Thick fish fillets suit this recipe admirably.

Serve hot, straight from the oven, and enjoy!

Chutney Broiled Fish

Fish broiled in coriander chutney batter

Serves 6

2 lbs. of any mild white fish fillets, cut into 3" x 3" pieces
(catfish and flounder work very well for this recipe.)
2 cloves garlic
2 cups chopped coriander leaves
4 hot green peppers
1 teaspoon whole cumin seeds
1 tablespoon chopped coconut
3/4 teaspoon ground turmeric
1/3 cup lemon juice
1/2 cup oil
salt to taste

Pat fish dry and set aside. Make a paste of all the other ingredients. Apply thickly on the fish, on both sides. Broil for 10 minutes on either side.

Serve very hot, straight from the oven.

Fish Curry in a Trice

Fish cooked in tomato and coriander

Serves 6

4 tablespoons oil
2 medium onions, chopped fine
2 cloves garlic, chopped
1 tablespoon chopped fresh ginger
3 medium tomatoes, chopped
2 tablespoons ground coriander seeds
2 teaspoons ground turmeric
salt to taste
1 tablespoon ground cumin seeds
2 cups water
2 lbs. of any mild white fish fillets, cut into 3" x 2" pieces
1 cup chopped fresh coriander

Heat the oil in a 6-quart saucepan on high heat. Add the onions, garlic and ginger. Fry for 2-3 minutes.

Add all the other ingredients EXCEPT the water, fish, and fresh coriander. Fry well.

Add the water. Bring to a boil.

Add the fish and the coriander; bring to a good boil again; cover; and cook on medium heat for 15 minutes.

Serve hot.

MACHHERE JHOL

An appetizing and delicate fish curry from the land of fish lovers, Bengal.

Serves 4

2 large tomatoes, coarsely chopped
1 tablespoon ground turmeric
2 teaspoons ground cumin seeds
salt to taste
2 cups water
1 cup oil
2 lbs. of any mild white fish, in thick fillets, cut into 2" x
    2" pieces
1/2 teaspoon mustard seeds
1/2 teaspoon whole cumin seeds
1/4 teaspoon whole fennel seeds, lightly crushed
1/2 teaspoon black cumin seeds
1/4 teaspoon fenugreek seeds

Gravy: In a 4-quart saucepan bring the tomatoes, tur-meric, ground cumin seed, salt and water to a boil.

Set aside.

In a non-stick frying pan, heat the oil on high heat.

Fry the fish, 4-5 pieces at a time, until golden.

Lift fish from the frying pan and place it in the gravy.

Add the mustard seeds, cumin seeds, fennel seeds, black cumin seeds and fenugreek seeds to the oil in the frying pan. Stir fry on high heat for a few seconds. Add the entire contents of the frying pan to the fish. Cook the fish on medium high for 10 minutes.

Serve hot.

VEGETARIAN

PANEER DO PIAZA

Homemade cottage cheese cubes, deep fried, and cooked in a tomato onion gravy.

Serves 8-10

To make PANEER or cottage cheese

  1/2 gallon whole milk
  2 lbs whole milk yoghurt
  1 cup lemon juice

Bring the milk to a good boil on high heat in a heavy 8-quart saucepan.

Mix the yoghurt and lemon juice well. Pour into the boiling milk.

Stir at once, only once, gently and slowly.

Shut off heat after a minute.

The milk should curdle. The water should separate from the milk solids and should be a light yellow color.

Cover and leave for half an hour.

Then, place a thin muslin-type material, such as a fine quality men's large handkerchief, over a large colander. Place the colander in a sink or over another 8 quart saucepan (Figure 7, page 88). Pour the curdled mixture into the cloth so that all the liquid drains off through the colander, leaving the cheese in the cloth. This should take a couple of minutes.

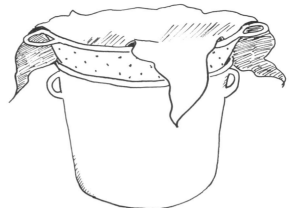

**HANDKERCHIEF
ON COLANDER
COLANDER ON
SAUCEPAN**
Figure 7

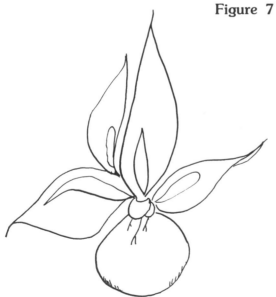

**CHEESE TIED
UP IN
HANDKERCHIEF**
Figure 8

HANGING CHEESE
Figure 9

Next, run cold water over the cheese for a minute. Allow all the liquid to drain off. Then tie up the cheese in the cloth, very tightly, so that some more liquid is drained off (Figure 8, page 88). Hang the cheese in the cloth for half an hour to drain off any remaining moisture (Figure 9, page 88).

Next, place the cheese on its side, on a board, so that the knot is on the side. Place another board on it, and then a heavy weight on the board, to press and squeeze out any moisture that might still be left in the cheese.

After 30 minutes, gently open up the cloth and place the cheese on a cutting board. If it is still warm, leave it until it cools completely. Then you can cut it into cubes about 2" x 2" x 1".

To fry PANEER

   1 cup oil

Heat the oil on high heat in a non-stick frying pan. Fry the cubes of cheese until they are a light reddish color. When done, lift with a slotted spoon and place in a bowl.

Do 4 or 5 pieces at a time. If you place too many pieces in the frying pan at the same time, they may stick together. Set aside.

To cook **DO PIAZA** or twice-onioned (twice-onioned is twice blessed!) **PANEER**

   1/2 cup oil from the frying oil
   2 cups chopped onions

1 teaspoon finely chopped fresh ginger
2 cloves garlic, minced
2 medium tomatoes, chopped
1 tablespoon ground cumin seeds
1 tablespoon ground coriander seeds
1 cup sliced onions
1/4 teaspoon ground cayenne pepper
1/4 teaspoon cardamon seeds, crushed
1 tablespoon GARAM MASALA
4 cloves
a pinch of ground nutmeg
2 cups water
salt to taste
fried cheese from the previous recipe

Heat the oil in a 4-quart saucepan on high heat for 2 minutes. Add the chopped onions, ginger, and garlic. Fry until golden brown for about 5 minutes. Add all the remaining ingredients, EXCEPT the cheese. Stirring occasionally, cook for about 5 minutes, until a thick sauce is formed. Add the fried cheese, stir gently to avoid breaking the cheese cubes. Lower the heat to medium, cover, and cook for about 20 minutes.

Serve hot.

RASAM from Geetha

An appetizer made with lentils and tomatoes

Serves 6

1/2 cup lentils
3 cups water
2 cups water
2 teaspoons RASAM powder (from an Indian store)
1/2 teaspoon ground turmeric
1/2 teaspoon garlic flakes
1/4 teaspoon tamarind paste
salt to taste
3 medium tomatoes, chopped
1-1/2 cups water
1 tablespoon GHEE
1 teaspoon mustard seeds
1 teaspoon whole cumin seeds
1/2 cup chopped fresh coriander

Cook the lentils in 3 cups of water in a covered saucepan until soft.

In a 4-quart saucepan, bring the 2 cups of water, RASAM powder, turmeric, garlic flakes, tamarind, salt, and tomatoes to a boil. Cook on medium high heat for 20 minutes.

Add the DAL; cook for 3 minutes. Add 1-1/2 cups of water, and continue to cook on medium high.

Heat up the GHEE. Add the mustard and cumin seeds; fry for a few seconds; add to the DAL. Add the coriander, boil once, and serve piping hot.

Delicious Everyday DAL

Serves 4-6

1 cup lentils
6 cups water
salt to taste
3 ripe, medium tomatoes, chopped
1 large onion, finely chopped
2 garlic cloves, minced
2 tablespoons finely chopped fresh ginger
4 tablespoons GHEE
1 teaspoon ground turmeric
1 teaspoon whole cumin seeds
2 dry red hot peppers
1/2 cup chopped fresh coriander

Bring all ingredients, EXCEPT fresh coriander, to a boil on high heat. Reduce heat to low, and cook until the DAL is tender. This should take 20-30 minutes, depending on which DAL you use.

When DAL is done, sprinkle coriander on top, stir and serve hot.

MOONG DAL

Serves 4-6

1 cup yellow split MOONG DAL
1 teaspoon ground turmeric
6 cups water
3 hot green peppers, halved
4 cloves
1 tablespoon curry leaves
salt to taste
4 tablespoons butter
1/2 teaspoon whole cumin seeds
2 cloves garlic, minced
1 tablespoon chopped fresh ginger

Bring the DAL, turmeric, water, peppers, cloves, curry leaves and salt to a boil on high heat. Lower heat to medium and cook till the DAL is tender. This should take 20-30 minutes.

Heat the butter in a small saucepan on high heat. Add the cumin, garlic and ginger; stir fry for 2 minutes. Add to the DAL; stir; and cook on medium high heat for 2 minutes more.

Serve hot.

MOTI MAHAL DAL

Serves 6

2 cups whole URAD DAL
One 15-oz can red kidney beans, washed in water and
    drained
8 cups water
6 tablespoons GHEE
4 hot green peppers, sliced
6 tablespoons heavy cream
1/2 cup tomato puree
1 onion, finely chopped
4 cloves garlic, finely chopped
1 tablespoon chopped fresh ginger
1 teaspoon whole cumin seeds

Bring the DAL, beans and water to a boil with 2 table-spoons GHEE and half the sliced peppers. Reduce heat to medium and cook for about 45 minutes or until DAL is tender.

Add the heavy cream. Let it boil for a minute or so. Add the tomato puree and remove from heat.

In a frying pan, heat the remaining GHEE on high heat.

Add the onion, garlic, ginger, remaining sliced peppers and cumin and fry for a couple of minutes. Add to the DAL and bring to a boil. Reduce heat to low and cook for 3 minutes.

Serve.

RAZMAH

Kidney beans for kings, made from the king of beans!

Serves 6-8

2 cups dry red kidney beans and
8 cups boiling water OR
Three 15-oz cans of kidney beans, washed and drained, plus
    1 cup water
2 tablespoons GHEE
1 teaspoon whole cumin seeds
1 cup sliced onions
2 cloves garlic, minced
1 tablespoon chopped fresh ginger
3 medium tomatoes, chopped
1 tablespoon ground cumin seeds
1 tablespoon ground coriander seeds
1 teaspoon ground turmeric
1/4 teaspoon ground cayenne pepper
salt to taste
3 hot green peppers
1/2 cup chopped fresh coriander

If you are cooking beans from scratch, clean and wash the beans. Place in a 4-quart saucepan. Pour the boiling water over the beans, and soak them in that water overnight.

The next day, bring the beans to a boil in the same water. Reduce heat to low, and cook to desired tenderness.

This may take an hour or more. If the water dries up as you cook, you can add more water and cook until the beans are done. (This method is not required for canned beans.)

OR you can use the canned beans and the cup of water. From now on the procedure is the same for both types of beans. Set aside the beans.

In a 4-quart saucepan, heat the GHEE on medium high heat.

Add the whole cumin seeds, and stir fry for a few seconds.

Add the onions, garlic, and ginger; fry until reddish. Add the tomatoes, ground cumin, ground coriander, turmeric, cayenne pepper, and salt; fry for a couple of minutes until a thick sauce is formed. Add the kidney beans and green peppers. Stir, bring to a boil, add the fresh coriander, and cook for 5 minutes.

Serve.

Curried Chick Peas from Ushaji

Serves 8

> 2 cups dry chick peas, soaked overnight in 4 cups water
> 4 more cups water OR
> Three 16-oz cans chick peas (washed with cold water and
>   drained), plus 1 cup water
> 3 tablespoons oil
> 2 teaspoons whole cumin seeds
> 2 teaspoons crushed anise seeds
> 1 tablespoon ground coriander seeds

1/2 teaspoon ginger powder
4 black cardamon pods, crushed well
1 cup tomato puree
1 teaspoon tamarind paste
1 tablespoon dry mint powder
salt to taste

For chick peas soaked in water: Bring the soaked peas with the water, plus the additional 1 cups of water to a boil in a 4-quart saucepan. Lower heat to medium; cover; and cook for an hour until tender.

OR use the canned chick peas plus the cup of water. From now on the procedure is the same for both types of chick peas.

Set aside the chick peas.

Heat the oil in a 4-quart saucepan, on high heat. Add all the other ingredients, EXCEPT the chick peas.

Stir fry for a few seconds. Add the chick peas, bring to a boil, reduce heat to low, cover; and cook for 20 minutes.

Serve.

Garlic Cabbage from Calcutta

Lovely with hot CHAPPATIS or rice!

Serves 6

6 tablespoons oil
6 hot green peppers, finely chopped
> You may reduce the number of peppers for mildness,
> but at least 4 peppers, seeds and all, are required for
> this recipe.

5 cloves garlic, minced
1 medium-sized cabbage, washed and drained thoroughly,
> cut into thin strips as for cole slaw; the strips should
> be as long as possible

salt to taste

In a 6-quart saucepan, heat the oil on high heat. Add the peppers and garlic, and stir fry briskly for a few seconds until golden. Add the cabbage and salt, and stir well until all ingredients are mixed thoroughly. This should take a couple of minutes.

Cook for 2 minutes. Turn off heat, and cover for 5 minutes before you serve. The cabbage should be a little crunchy when done, not raw and not too soft.

Serve at once.

BHINDI ALOO

Crisp, curried okra and potatoes

Serves 6

1 lb. fresh okra
1 lb. medium potatoes, cut like home fries, preferably red
   potatoes with skin left on
3/4 cup oil
1 tablespoon ground coriander seeds
1 tablespoon ground cumin seeds
1/2 tablespoon ground turmeric
1 tablespoon GARAM MASALA
salt to taste
Optional: Half a cup chopped fresh coriander for seasoning

Wash and drain vegetables thoroughly. The okra, particularly, should be washed and drained well in advance so that it is completely dry when ready to be cooked. When the okra is completely dry, cut off and discard the stem ends.

Heat the oil in a heavy wok on high heat for a couple of minutes.

Add the vegetables.

Stir fry for about 5 minutes.

Add all the other ingredients EXCEPT the coriander, and stir well. Lower heat to medium, cover, and cook until potatoes and okra are done; i.e., tender.

Sprinkle with chopped coriander, if you like coriander as much as I do!!

Serve.

Broccoli Rabe HAAK

A quick, delicious and nutritious recipe

Serves 4

1 lb. broccoli rabe or rabi
6 tablespoons oil
1/2 teaspoon dry HING powder
salt to taste
10 small, dry, hot red peppers
1-1/2 cups water

Wash and cut rabe stalks in half. Remove any seeds or flowers.

Heat the oil in a 4-quart saucepan on high heat for a couple of minutes. Remove from heat.

Add the HING, salt, peppers and water.

Return saucepan to heat.

Add rabe; stir; bring to a boil; lower heat to medium high; cover and cook for 10 minutes.

Remove cover immediately after the 10 minutes are over to retain the appetizing green color of the leaves.

Serving suggestion for a different and refreshing taste: serve with hot boiled rice and plain yoghurt!

Hot Broccoli

Serves 4-6

5 tablespoons oil
1 tablespoon crushed peppers
salt to taste
1 head of broccoli, washed, drained, cut into pieces, stalks
    and all

Heat the oil on high heat in a 4-quart saucepan for 2 minutes.

Add the peppers, salt, and broccoli. Stir fry for 2 minutes.

Reduce heat to medium high; cook, covered, for 5 minutes.

Serve.

Turnips and kohlrabi can also be cooked this way. However, you may need to add a cup or two of water to the vegetables after stir frying, since they take longer to cook than broccoli.

Kalpana's DOSA BHAJI

Served as a potato filling for South Indian crepes called DOSAS, BHAJI is delightful even with rice or bread.

Serves 6

4 tablespoons oil
1 teaspoon mustard seeds
1 teaspoon CHANNA DAL

1 teaspoon URAD DAL
3 cloves
10 curry leaves
2 tablespoons chopped fresh ginger
3 hot green peppers, coarsely chopped
2 small sliced onions
4 boiled, large potatoes, broken into chunks
salt to taste
1/2 teaspoon ground turmeric
3 medium tomatoes, chopped
1/2 teaspoon ground cayenne pepper
1 cup water
1/4 cup chopped fresh coriander

In a 4-quart saucepan, heat the oil on high heat for 2 minutes. Reduce heat to medium high.

Add the mustard seeds, and stir fry for a couple of seconds.

Add the CHANNA and URAD DAL, and stir fry for a few seconds.

Add the cloves, curry leaves, ginger, green peppers and the onions. Fry until the onions are soft. Add the potatoes, fry for a few more minutes.

Add the salt, turmeric, tomatoes and cayenne pepper. Pour in the water; stir well. Reduce heat to medium, cover, and cook for about 10 minutes. Sprinkle the coriander on top.

Serve.

Eggplant and Tomato Curry

*Try to use garden fresh baby eggplants for this prep-
aration, which is very similar to a ratatouille.*

Serves 4-6

3 medium tomatoes, very preferably those ripened on the
    vine
3 hot green peppers
1 teaspoon ground turmeric
1/2 teaspoon ginger powder
1/2 teaspoon ground fennel seeds
1/2 teaspoon ground cumin seeds
3 cloves
1 cup water
1/2 teaspoon ground cayenne pepper
salt to taste
1 lb. small or baby eggplants
1 cup oil

Gravy: Cut each tomato into 6 pieces. Place the tomatoes
and all the other ingredients, EXCEPT the eggplants and
the oil, in a 4-quart saucepan. Cook on medium high heat
for 5-7 minutes or until the tomatoes have cooked down
a bit. Set aside.

Wash and wipe the eggplants dry so that when you fry
them, there is very little spattering. Cut into quarters
lengthwise. If the eggplants are long, cut into quarters
lengthwise and then once across so that you have 8
pieces.

Heat the oil on high heat in a wok for a couple of minutes. Add the eggplants, and stir fry for about 5 minutes until the eggplants start turning a little reddish in places. Pour eggplants and oil into the tomato mixture. Stir a bit to cover eggplants with the gravy.

Return saucepan to heat, and cook uncovered on medium high for another 5 minutes.

Serve.

Cauliflower and Peas Curry

Serves 6

3/4 cup oil, or GHEE
1/2 teaspoon whole cumin seeds
2 medium onions, sliced
3 cloves garlic, minced
2 tablespoons finely chopped fresh ginger
3 medium tomatoes, chopped
2 teaspoons ground coriander seeds
1 teaspoon ground turmeric
2 teaspoons ground cumin seeds
1 teaspoon ground cayenne pepper
2 black cardamons, crushed well
salt to taste
1 medium cauliflower, cut into 3" long florets, washed and
        drained thoroughly, so that it is dry
2-1/2 cups frozen peas
1 cup chopped fresh coriander

Heat the oil or GHEE on high heat in a wok. Add the whole cumin, and stir until it sizzles briskly for a few seconds. Add the onions, garlic and ginger; stir fry till a golden brown. Add the tomatoes and continue frying for about 5 minutes until you have a reddish paste. Add the ground coriander, turmeric, cumin, pepper, cardamon, and salt; continue stir frying until all the spices are well blended in the paste. Add the cauliflower and fry well. This should take about 8 minutes on high heat. Stir off and on to prevent the mixture from sticking to the bottom of the wok.

Add the peas, stir, lower heat to medium high heat; cover; and cook till the cauliflower is done to desired tenderness. This should take about 5 minutes. Just before serving, sprinkle the fresh coriander on top.

Avoid using any water to cook cauliflower if you want it to be crunchy and not too soft. However, if you feel the gravy is drying up too fast and the cauliflower is likely to burn, add a quarter cup of water.

Green Beans Curry from Aruna, a Southern Belle
Serves 6

> 1 lb. green beans, cut into one inch pieces
> salt to taste
> 1/2 cup water
> 2 tablespoons oil

1/2 tablespoon mustard seeds
a few curry leaves
1/2 tablespoon grated fresh ginger
1 small onion, finely chopped
1/2 cup grated fresh coconut

Bring the beans, salt, and water to a boil in a medium saucepan on high heat. Cover; lower heat to medium, and cook for 10 minutes. Drain off water and set the beans aside.

In a 4-quart saucepan, heat the oil on high. Add the mustard seeds, curry leaves, ginger and onion. Fry for a couple of minutes. Add beans, and stir fry for a minute. Add the grated coconut; stir; and remove from heat.

Serve hot.

Tulli's DAM ALOO

Smothered whole potatoes in a yoghurt gravy

About 6 medium DAM ALOO

1 lb. medium potatoes
water to cover and boil potatoes
2 cups oil
1 medium onion, chopped
half a cup yoghurt
1 teaspoon ground cayenne pepper
1 teaspoon ground fennel seeds
1/2 teaspoon ginger powder

1/4 teaspoon ground cumin seeds
6 cloves
salt to taste
1 cup water

Boil the potatoes in a saucepan until done. Drain off water. Allow potatoes to cool. Pare off skin and perforate potatoes all over, deeply, with a tooth pick. Set potatoes aside. Heat the oil in a wok on high heat until very hot. Deep fry the potatoes until they become reddish brown all over. This may take a while. The potatoes are not done until they turn reddish all over. Remove with a slotted spoon and set aside. Remove wok from heat.

In a 4-quart saucepan, heat 3 tablespoons of the oil from the wok on medium high heat. Add the onion, and fry until light brown. Mix the yoghurt with the cayenne pepper and stir in with the onion. Add the fennel, ginger, cumin, cloves, and salt in quick succession; stir. Add the water, then the potatoes. Stir gently, but well. Bring to a boil. Cover. Reduce heat to low, and cook for 10 minutes.

Serve hot.

RAITA

My Mother-in-Law's Fresh
CHUGANDHAR RAITA

Beetroot and yoghurt delight

Serves 6

4 beets, medium size, boiled, peeled and diced
1 onion, finely chopped
1 hot green pepper, very finely chopped
1 tablespoon grated fresh ginger
salt to taste
1/4 teaspoon whole cumin seeds
1/4 teaspoon ground black pepper
1/2 cup chopped fresh coriander; save a pinch for garnish
2 cups yoghurt
1 pint sour cream

Wash beets thoroughly under running water to remove some of the color. Drain well.

Mix all the ingredients; garnish with a pinch of the fresh coriander.

Chill and serve.

The yoghurt and sour cream acquire a glamorous pink color that really brightens up a dinner table.

Orange Cucumber RAITA
Serves 6

1 cucumber
salt to taste
2 cups plain, whole milk yoghurt
1 cup sour cream
One 15-oz. can mandarin oranges, drained
1/2 cup chopped fresh coriander

Wash and peel the cucumber, cut in half, lengthwise. Spoon out the seeds and discard them. Grate cucumber and sprinkle with salt. Set aside for an hour.

Mix the yoghurt and the sour cream well.

Add oranges. Squeeze out the water from the cucumber by hand.

Add the cucumber to the yoghurt mixture.

Mix well.

Garnish with coriander.

Serve chilled.

MINT RAITA

2 cups yoghurt
1/2 cup sour cream
mint chutney
a few leaves fresh mint

Mix all the ingredients, EXCEPT the mint leaves, well.

Garnish with the mint leaves; chill; and serve.

SALADS, CHUTNEYS AND A PICKLE!

Traditional Everyday Salad

This salad goes well with TANDOORI meats.

2 large onions, sliced
2 beets boiled until tender, cooled, peeled and sliced
1 cucumber, peeled and sliced
1 large tomato, sliced
1 fresh lime, sliced
2 hot green peppers, sliced
6 scallions, cleaned, cut to 5" length, then halved lengthwise
2 tablespoons vinegar
salt and pepper to taste

Place the onions in a layer on a large plate. Next, place the beets on top in a layer, then the cucumber, then the tomato slices, and last of all the sliced lime. Scatter the green peppers on top. Arrange the scallions in a pattern on the vegetables. Sprinkle with vinegar, salt and pepper.

Chill and serve.

Mahavir KA CACHUMBER KA SALAAD

A finely minced salad, CACHUMBER is a perfect accompaniment to a rich PULLAO or BIRYANI. In fact, it can be the only other accompaniment, along with yoghurt, if you are in the mood for a light meal. The name CACHUMBER SALAAD, originates from the Indian chef's inability, presumably, to pronounce the Britisher's favorite salad vegetable, cucumber. Now CACHUMBER means a finely chopped salad, and the word has found a place in verbal arguments in which the parties are threatening each other with dire consequences!

    1 large cucumber
    1 large onion
    1 large tomato
    salt to taste
    1 tablespoon lemon juice
    1 cup chopped fresh coriander

Dice the cucumber, onion, and tomato very fine, by halving, then cutting into strips and then cutting across. Add the salt, lemon juice, and coriander. Mix well.

Chill and serve.

Mint Chutney

Refreshing!

    fresh mint, about 3 cups of leaves, washed
    1/2 onion
    1 tablespoon chopped fresh ginger
    4 green hot peppers
    salt to taste
    1/4 cup lemon juice
    a little water to blend, about 3 tablespoons

Grind all ingredients together in a blender.

Serve with KABABS and SAMOSAS.

Saryu's Date Chutney

12 ounces pitted dates
2 tablespoons brown sugar
2 tablespoons tamarind paste
pinch salt
1-1/2 cups water

Puree all the ingredients together in a blender.

Serve chilled or at room temperature.

Fresh Chutney

1 large ripe tomato
6 hot green peppers
2 cups chopped fresh coriander
1 small onion, coarsely chopped
2 cloves garlic
2 tablespoons lime juice
salt to taste

Puree all the ingredients together in a blender.

Chill and serve.

Walnut Mint Chutney

1 dozen walnuts, shelled and soaked in water for 24 hours
2 hot green peppers
1 cup fresh mint leaves, washed and drained
1/3 cup water
salt to taste
3 tablespoons sour cream (optional)

Grind all the ingredients together in a blender.

For a variation, add 3 tablespoons of sour cream and mix well.

Chill and serve.

My Favorite Cooked Pickle

Sweet and sour, this pickle is almost like a curry!!!

1-1/2 lbs. raw mangoes, or hot green peppers; very, very
     fresh, without any bruises
1/2 cup whole cumin seeds
1/4 cup whole fenugreek seeds
1 cup wine vinegar
1/2 cup chopped fresh ginger
12 large cloves of garlic
1 medium onion, coarsely chopped
1-1/2 teaspoon salt
1 cup sugar
1 tablespoon ground cayenne pepper
1 cup oil

Wash the mangoes (or peppers), and dry them completely. Chop into small pieces and set aside.

Grind the cumin and fenugreek seeds well in the vinegar. Add all the other ingredients EXCEPT the oil and the mangoes (or peppers), and grind until a fine puree is made.

Heat the oil in a wok, on high heat, until it almost starts to smoke. Add the puree, very carefully, and stir fry briskly for 3-4 minutes.

Add the mangoes (or peppers), and stir fry briskly for another 3-4 minutes. Remove from heat. Allow to cool completely.

Store in an air tight bottle in the refrigerator.

Always use a clean, dry, spoon when serving the pickle, as this keeps the pickle from spoiling.

DESSERTS

East meets West in Mango Souffle

An "exceptional" recipe from Lily.

Serves 8

2 small envelopes unflavored gelatin
2 cups mango puree
a small pinch of saffron
4 egg whites
1/4 cup sugar
1/2 pint heavy whipping cream
8 green pistachios, ground
seeds of 2 cardamon pods, crushed to a powder

Stir the gelatin into one cup mango puree. Stirring all the time, cook over medium heat till the gelatin dissolves. Remove from heat. Add the saffron and the other cup of mango puree, stir well. Chill in the refrigerator, until mounds form in the puree when you lift it with a spoon. This should take about 15 minutes. Remove from refrigerator.

Whip up the egg whites with 1/4 cup of sugar until stiff, and fold them into the puree.

Whip up the cream. Reserve a dollop for decoration. Fold the rest of the whipped cream into the mango puree. Pour into a glass dish.

Sprinkle with pistachios and cardamon. Top with the dollop of whipped cream.

Chill for at least 3 hours, or until it sets.

Serve.

RASMALAI a la Vini

RASMALAI, translated literally, means cream sauce. This is a dessert made of cottage cheese, cream, sugar and nuts. In India, the cheese is shaped into balls and soaked in cream after being cooked. Then it is chilled, garnished and served. This delicious version is a shortcut.

Serves 8

    2 lbs. ricotta cheese
    1/2 cup sugar
    1 pint half and half
    a pinch of saffron
    1/4 teaspoon cardamon seeds, finely crushed
    1/2 cup blanched almonds, finely slivered
    2 tablespoons crushed green pistachios

Mix the cheese and sugar very well. Spread out on a deep 9"x 12" baking tray. Bake at 350 degrees for 35 minutes or until it sets. It should not brown. Remove from oven. Cool at room temperature and cut into 2 inch squares. Place in a dessert bowl.

Mix the other ingredients, EXCEPT the pistachios, well in a separate dish. Pour over the squares. Decorate with pistachios.

Chill for 2-3 hours before serving.

KULFI GALI WALI

A centuries old ice-cream, courtesy of Ushi

To serve 12

One 12-oz can evaporated milk
1 pint heavy whipping cream
One 14-oz can condensed sweetened milk
2 slices white bread, edges trimmed
20 almonds, blanched and peeled
1/2 cup green pistachios
a pinch of saffron, soaked for 10 minutes in 1 teaspoon
    water
1/2 teaspoon cardamon seeds, crushed well

Put everything in the blender. Run the blender for about
a minute until everything is well pureed. After turning off
the blender, mix the ingredients with a spatula to make
sure the nuts are not at the bottom. Run the blender once
again for a minute. Make sure the nuts are well pureed
with the other ingredients. Pour into popsicle molds.
Freeze overnight or for at least 12 hours. Makes approximately 12 molds.

GHULAB (Rose) JAMUNS from Geetha

"Rose Berries" in a fragrant syrup

To make about 50 GHULAB JAMUNS, about 3 to a serving

4 cups water
1 tablespoon rose water
3 cups sugar
a pinch of saffron

2-1/2 cups dry milk powder
1/2 cup all purpose flour
1/8 teaspoon baking soda
about 1-1/2 cups heavy cream, enough to make dough
about 50 cardamon seeds
2 cups oil

Bring the water, rose water, and sugar to a boil. Add the saffron. Remove from heat and set aside near the wok in which you plan to fry the GHULAB JAMUNS.

Mix the milk powder, flour, soda and heavy cream well. Knead until a soft dough is made. Take a teaspoon of the dough; place one cardamon seed in it and make a small ball.

Make balls with the rest of the dough similarly. Set aside. It is a good idea to make all the balls and then fry them in batches of 8. It takes a minute or two to fry the JAMUNS when the oil is ready.

In a wok, heat the oil on medium high heat for 10 minutes. When ready, fry the GHULAB JAMUNS, until they turn brownish.

Remove with a slotted spoon and transfer to the syrup which should still be quite warm.

If, for some reason, the syrup has become entirely cold, heat it up a little before you place the JAMUNS in it.

This is a good recipe for the winter AND summer. In the winter GHULAB JAMUNS are usually served heated. In the summer they can be served chilled or at room temperature.

BHAPPA DOI, the way Ammi makes it

A steamed yoghurt dessert favorite from Bengal

Serves 6

One 14-oz can condensed sweetened milk
1-1/4 cup thick yoghurt
2 tablespoons blanched, slivered almonds
1/4 teaspoon crushed cardamon
1/8 teaspoon ground nutmeg

Mix all the ingredients well and steam in a covered pan, about the size of a 9-inch pie dish, for about half an hour until the DOI solidifies. Remove from heat, and set aside to cool. Next, chill in the refrigerator for at least 4 hours. When chilled, cut into 2 inch pieces.

Serve chilled.

Two pieces or more to a serving.

Agha Shahid Ali's Easy-as-Pie KHIR, OR, a Shortcut to a Heavenly Rice Pudding

This amazingly simple and delectable version of KHIR is a concoction of a friend of mine. His guests always rave over his KHIR. You have to try this recipe to find out why!

Serves 6

1/2 cup good quality rice
5 cups water
One 12-oz can evaporated milk
One 14-oz can condensed, sweetened milk

a pinch of saffron
6 crushed cardamon pods
1-1/2 cups in all of almonds, brazil nuts, cashew nuts and
    dates, all finely slivered
1/2 cup raisins

Bring the rice and water to a boil. Reduce heat to the lowest point; cover; and cook until the rice is very soft and sticky. This should take about 30 minutes or so. Remove from heat. Set aside to cool.

When cool, mash with a potato masher.

Add all the other ingredients, mix well, and bring to a boil in a very heavy saucepan. Stir, lower heat to the lowest point, and simmer for 10 minutes.

Serve hot or chilled.

NANKATAI or Indian Biscuits

Makes about 4 dozen NANKATAI.

8 ounces butter
1-1/2 cups sugar
2 teaspoons water
1/2 teaspoon baking soda
1/2 teaspoon cardamon seeds, powdered
2 cups all purpose flour
a few green pistachios, slivered

Soften butter at room temperature. Add the sugar, water and soda. Blend this in a food processor until creamy.

Mix the cardamon with the flour well.

Blend the flour mixture, one tablespoon at a time, into the butter mixture, in a food processor till you achieve a soft, smooth dough.

Form into small balls by the spoonful, with the palms of your hands (See CHAPPATIS, page 42). Decorate each ball with a sliver of pistachio.

Preheat the oven to 300 degrees. When ready, place the NANKATAI on cookie sheets and bake like cookies for about 15 minutes. The NANKATAI are done when they start to turn a little brown at the bottom.

Remove from oven and allow to cool at room temperature.

Enjoy!

SNACKS

SAMOSA

A standard snack at tea time. SAMOSA is a deep fried, spring roll type of savory, usually stuffed with potatoes and peas. Cooked, spiced ground meat can be used instead of potatoes.

To make 20

For the dough:

2 cups all purpose flour
1-1/2 teaspoon whole cumin seeds
1/4 teaspoon ground anise
a pinch of salt
1/2 cup vegetable shortening
about 1/3 cup chilled water to make dough
1/2 cup extra flour to roll out the wrappers
2 cups vegetable shortening to deep fry the SAMOSAS

Mix the flour, cumin, anise and salt. Add the shortening, and rub into the flour mixture, until little granules are formed. Add the water, a little at a time, until a stiff dough is made. Knead well for a few minutes; cover; and keep in the refrigerator for a couple of hours before rolling out the wrappers.

When ready to roll, make a "log" out of the dough, as described for CHAPPATIS (page 42). Cut into 10 pieces.

Make a ball out of one piece with your palms, as you would for CHAPPATIS. Flatten the ball on the counter.

127

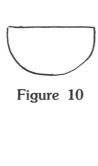

Figure 10

Figure 11

Figure 12

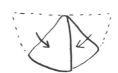

Figure 13

Figure 14

With the help of a little dry flour, roll out a flat, round shape, about 7" in diameter. Follow the basic rules for rolling out the CHAPPATIS.

With a knife or pizza cutter, cut the rolled out circle in half.

Take one half with the curved side towards you as indicated in Figure 10, page 128.

Place a tablespoon of the filling in the center (Figure 11, page 128).

Moisten the curved edges, by dipping your finger in water, and running over the edge.

Next, fold the right half over the filling (Figure 12, page 128). Moisten top edge.

Bring the left fold over the folded right half and press down gently (Figure 13, page 128).

Moisten the base of the triangle; fold up at the edge and top; and press down well with a fork or fingertips, as you do with pastry, to seal it (Figure 14, page 128).

This ensures that the filling does not stand a chance of spilling out. Make all the SAMOSAS and set them out on a tray.

To fry: Heat the 2 cups of vegetable shortening in a wok on high heat.

Reduce heat to medium high.

When the shortening has been on medium high for 5 minutes, drop a pinch of dough into it. If the dough rises to the top at once, the oil is ready.

Deep fry the SAMOSAS, four at a time. Fry on one side until they turn a golden brown. Then turn them over, and fry on the other side.

When done, lift the SAMOSAS with a slotted spoon and place them on 3-4 layers of paper towels. The towels soak up excess oil.

SAMOSAS can be eaten hot or cold. To re-heat, warm SAMOSAS in the oven.

Serve with ketchup or chutney.

Filling for Samosas:

> 6 medium potatoes, boiled until done, peeled, broken into coarse chunks
> 1 large onion, very finely chopped
> 2 tablespoons finely chopped fresh ginger
> 2 cloves garlic, minced
> 1 cup peas, frozen (or precooked by boiling and draining off the water)
> 1 teaspoon crushed red pepper, less to taste
> 2 tablespoons ground coriander seeds
> 1 teaspoon ground cumin seeds
> 2 cups chopped fresh coriander
> salt to taste

NOTE: Instead of the potato filling, you can use the cooked meat from the KHULLA KEEMA recipe (pg. 68). All you need to add to the ground meat is fresh coriander. Make sure there is no gravy. If the meat filling does not adhere, add a couple of boiled mashed potatoes to it, and mix it well, before stuffing the SAMOSAS.

Mix all the ingredients for the filling well by hand so that they stick together like a dough.

The most important thing to keep in mind is that the filling should be absolutely dry. The presence of any liquid makes it impossible to seal the SAMOSA

Make a little ball of the filling, and place it in the wrapper.

Fold, crimp and fry as described above.

Zarina's Knock out Corn VADE

Deep fried corn savouries

Serves 8

One 20-oz packet of frozen corn, completely thawed in the
    packet
2 tablespoons chopped fresh ginger
4 cloves garlic
salt to taste
2 teaspoons sugar
3 hot green peppers
1/2 teaspoon ground turmeric
1/2 teaspoon ground cayenne pepper
3 tablespoons all purpose flour
1 egg
3 tablespoons instant cream of wheat
2 cups oil for deep frying

Blend all the ingredients, EXCEPT the oil, in an electric blender until a paste is made. This may take a while, but it will eventually be reduced to a paste in the blender! You may have to turn off the blender and mix the ingredients with a spatula, remove the spatula, cover the blender and start the blending process again a couple of times, before you are successful.

Heat the oil in a wok, on high heat, until a drop of the paste begins to sizzle and fry briskly at once. Remove the drop of paste.

Drop the paste by the spoonful, six at a time, into the oil. The VADE are done as soon as they turn reddish all over.

Remove the VADE with a slotted spoon and place on 3-4 layers of paper towels for a minute or two.

Serve hot.

The corn MUST thaw completely before you blend it, or it does not make a paste.

Fantastically simple and simply fantastic!!

Fish KABABS

Fish cakes, made the Indian way!

To make about 25 KABABS

2 lbs. of any mild white fish fillet (Cod works the best for this recipe)
4 cups water to boil the fish

2 large boiled potatoes, skins removed
2 eggs
1 tablespoon whole cumin seeds
1 tablespoon ground coriander seeds
1 teaspoon ground cayenne pepper
1 cup finely minced onion
1 tablespoon finely minced fresh ginger
salt to taste
1 cup chopped fresh coriander
4 hot green peppers, finely minced
2 teaspoons GARAM MASALA
1 cup oil to fry the fish

Boil the fish, covered, in the water on medium high heat until done. This should take about 10 minutes.

Drain off the water, and allow the fish to cool.

When cool, mix the fish well with all other ingredients, EXCEPT the oil.

Knead for a couple of minutes until soft, taking care that no chunks are left. Make fish cakes about 2 inches in diameter and 1/2 inches in thickness. Set aside on a tray. Heat oil in a non-stick frying pan on medium high heat. When the oil is ready, fry 4-5 cakes at a time. Turn over when one side is reddish brown. Then fry until the other side is reddish brown.

The cakes should be fried crisp on both sides.

Place on 4 layers of paper towels for a few minutes before serving. The towels will soak up excess oil.

Serve hot, with ketchup or fresh chutney.

Menus

The following pages list possible combinations for meals, from recipes in this book. These are only suggestions. You have to keep in mind that there should be

    a) rice, and/ or one of the breads and
    b) a vegetarian or a non-vegetarian entree.

To make it a little elaborate, you could add

    c) a DAL and
    d) a salad.

To make it a little more elaborate, also add

    e) RAITA and
    f) dessert.

If you want to serve a terribly sophisticated meal, add two or three entrees and/or a PULLAO.

It really is up to you. I have just combined items that I think would taste good together. You can delete or add items to make a menu that suits you better.

RASAM can be served as an appetizer before meals.

SAMOSAS, Corn VADE and Fish KABABS can be served with a CHUTNEY, as snacks.

Vegetarian Meals

1. Plain Rice, Broccoli Rabe, Eggplant and Tomato Curry, MOONG DAL, and KHIR.

2. Plain Rice, DAM ALOO, DAL, Garlic Cabbage, and RASMALAI.
3. Plain Rice, Hot Broccoli, RAZMAH, Mint RAITA, and BHAPPA DOI.
4. Plain Rice, DAL, Broccoli Rabe, Fresh CHUTNEY, and GHULAB JAMUN.
5. Plain Rice, PANEER DO PIAZA, DAM ALOO, CACHUM-BAR KA SALAD, and KULFI.
6. Vegetable PULLAO, RAZMAH, Cucumber RAITA, and KULFI.
7. Vegetable PULLAO, PANEER DO PIAZA, BHINDI ALOO, BEETROOT RAITA, and GHULAB JAMUN.
8. Vegetable PULLAO, MOTI MAHAL DAL, Green Beans Curry, and Mango Souffle.
9. CHAPPATI, Cauliflower Curry, DAL, Orange Cucumber RAITA, and GHULAB JAMUN.
10. CHAPPATI, Garlic Cabbage, Chick Peas, and KHIR.
11. CHAPPATI, BHINDI ALOO, MOONG DAL, and KHIR.
12. Plain PARATHA, BHINDI ALOO, Cauliflower and Peas Curry, Mint RAITA, and GHULAB JAMUN.
13. Stuffed PARATHAS, Chick Peas, Hot Broccoli, Mint RAITA, and KHIR.
14. Stuffed PARATHA, RAZMAH, CACHUMBAR SALAD, and GHULAB JAMUN.
15. PURI, DOSA BHAJI, MOTI MAHAL DAL, CACHUMBER KA SALAD, and KHIR.
16. PURI, DOSA BHAJI, CHICK PEAS, CACHUMBER SALAD, and RASMALAI.
17. A grand vegetarian meal would include Vegetable PULLAO, PURIS, Cauliflower and Peas, PANEER DO PIAZA, BHINDI ALOO, MOTI MAHAL DAL, Everyday Salad, Mint RAITA and GHULAB JAMUN or RASMALAI.

Non-Vegetarian

1. Plain Rice, SHAMI, DAM ALOO, Hot Broccoli, and GHULAB JAMUN.
2. Plain Rice, Chicken Curry, Green Beans, DAL, and BHAPPA DOI.
3. Plain Rice, SHAMI, Hot Broccoli, Plain Yoghurt, and GHULAB JAMUN.
4. Plain Rice, PIAZ Chicken, DAL, Broccoli Rabe, and BHAPPA DOI.
5. Plain Rice, SAG GOSTH, Plain Yoghurt, Everyday Salad, and RASMALAI.
6. Plain Rice, KALIYA, Eggplant and Tomato Curry, RAZMAH, Orange Cucumber RAITA, and GHULAB JAMUN.
7. Plain Rice or Vegetable PULLAO, ROGHANJOSH, Green Beans Curry, Mint CHUTNEY, and GHULAB JAMUN.
8. Plain Rice, AWADHI DO PIAZA, BHINDI ALOO, DAL, Beetroot RAITA, and GHULAB JAMUN.
9. Plain Rice, CHUTNEY Broiled Fish, MOONG DAL, Garlic Cabbage, and BHAPPA DOI.
10. Plain Rice, VINDALOO, DOSA BHAJI, Green Beans, and Mango Souffle.
11. Plain Rice or Vegetable PULLAO, MACHHERE JHOL, MOONG DAL, Cauliflower and Peas Curry, CACHUMBAR KA SALAD, and BHAPPA DOI.
12. Vegetable PULLAO, TIKKA KABAB, Garlic Cabbage, DAL, and Mango Souffle.
13. Vegetable PULLAO, BHUNA Lamb, KHULLA KEEMA, Everyday Salad, and KULFI.
14. Vegetable PULLAO, Butter Chicken, CACHUMBER KA

SALAD, and KULFI.

15. Vegetable PULLAO, SHAHI KORMA, MOTI MAHAL DAL, CACHUMBER KA SALAD, and KULFI.

16. Vegetable PULLAO, TIKKA KABABS, RAZMAH, Orange Cucumber RAITA, and KULFI.

17. Lamb PULLAO, DAM ALOO, RAZMAH, Mint Raita, and Mango Souffle.

18. Lamb PULLAO, YAKHNI, RAZMAH, Broccoli Rabe, and KULFI.

19. A grand dinner from Kashmir would include Lamb PULLAO, ROGHANJOSH, KOFTE, YAKHNI, Broccoli Rabe HAAK, RAZMAH, Walnut Mint CHUTNEY, and RASMALAI.

20. Lamb PULLAO, TANDOORI Fish, Cauliflower and Peas Curry, and KULFI.

21. Lamb BIRYANI, CACHUMBAR KA SALAD, Mint RAITA, and KULFI.

22. Lamb BIRYANI, SHAHI KORMA, Beetroot RAITA, Every-day Salad, and GHULAB JAMUN.

23. Lamb BIRYANI, PIAZ Chicken, MOTI MAHAL DAL, BHIN-DI ALOO, Cucumber Orange Raita, and RASMALAI.

24. Lamb BIRYANI, TANDOORI Chicken, Caulifower and Peas Curry, CACHUMBAR KA SALAD, and RASMALAI.

25. KHICHDI, DAM ALOO, Walnut Mint CHUTNEY, and GHULAB JAMUN.

26. Plain PARATHA, KOFTE, CACHUMBAR KA SALAD, and RASMALAI.

27. CHAPPATI, Butter Chicken, MOTI MAHAL DAL, Every-day Salad, and KULFI.

This is not an exhaustive list by any means.

Welcome to Indian Cuisine!

Recipe Index:

BASIC RECIPES

RICE

BREADS

NON-VEGETARIAN

VEGETARIAN

Illustration Index: